For My Dear Sister in Spirit, So grateful our journeys have brought us here. Lots of Love – Amru

WE DANCE TO A WHISPERED VOICE

WE DANCE TO A WHISPERED VOICE:

A SHAMANIC AWAKENING
BY AMARI MAGDALENA

Other Books by Amari Magdalena

Awaken Your Inner Personas
Unbecoming Me
On Becoming Invisible
Blue Moons and Golden Suns
Shaman Talk

★Amaristar Productions
3353 Racine Street
#328
Bellingham WA 98226
Phone: 1-541-591-6503

© 2017 by Amari Magdalena All rights reserved.

No part of this material may be reproduced, stored in a retrieval system, or transmitted by any means without the written permission of the author.

First re-published by ★Amaristar Productions [04/28/17]

ISBN-13: 978-1530918713

ISBN-10: 1530918715

Printed in the United States of America

© Photographic Images exclusive property of Amari Magdalena.

Cover Design by Kayin J. Fields.

This book is printed on acid-free paper.

The views expressed in this work are solely those of the author and do not necessarily reflect the views of the publisher, and the publisher hereby disclaims any responsibility for them.

CONTENTS

Chapter I. Strange Happenings   Page 3

    Holy Spirit Visitations
    Seattle and Nature of the Soul
    Joseph's Angelic Presence

Chapter II. Magical Move   Page 11

    Mystical Call & Magical Move
    Aurora
    E'Star and Jessie

Chapter III. Entering Other Worlds   Page 19

    Magic Watch Band
    Miguel & Sarita
    Teleportation & Gaia
    Elena & Dance of the Curandera's in Abiquiu
    Taos Pueblo

Chapter IV. Phantasmagorical Period   Page 29

    11:11 Stargate
    Twelve Entities
    Calling Animals and Bionic Woman
    Elena Gallegos and Other Portals
    Time Lapse
    Plant Medicine
    Spelunking in Private Caves
    UFO's

Chapter V. Siren's Call Southeast-Atlanta Page 43

> Trail of Tears
> Universal Brotherhood and the Peace Circle
> Kituwah Festival in Ashville North Carolina
> Working with Weather
> Etowah Mounds
> Holistic School and Teaching
> Lesson in Discernment
> Florida

Chapter VI. Red Rocks Beckon-Sedona   Page 67

> Vortices
> Small Demonstrations of Power
> Illness
> Magical Path
> Birth of Earth Ceremony in Japan

Chapter VII. Sonoran Sunsets & Saguaro   Page 77

> Building a Practice
> Agua Caliente Park
> Sabino Canyon
> Radio Show
> Intensives & Sanctuary Cove

Chapter VIII. Heart of Texas   Page 85

> Austin Community College & Teaching
> Cross Roads Retreat Center and Other Places
> Peru and the Amaru Maru Portal

Chapter IX.   Land of Entrapment   Page 95

    Rancho De Las Barrancas, Pojoaque, NM
    Sophia Seminary
    Apprentices and Teaching

Chapter X.   High and Low Deserts   Page 101

    Prescott
    Back to Tucson
    2012 Birth of the New Earth
    Magdala Sanctuary
    Tubac Consciousness Group

Chapter XI.   Full Circle   Page 113

    Winds
    Ashland-Wrong Time, Wrong Place
    Bellingham-Home to the Sea

About the Author   Page 122

Glossary of Terms   Page 124

Recommendations   Page 125

Next Book   Page 127

INTRODUCTION

Deep within each of us lies a dormant dancer awaiting the call to oscillate to the soul's rhythm. Many sit in the balcony of their own lives awaiting the invitation of a sultry voice whispering, "*OK, you may begin.*" Others go through the motions of movement in a culture that has misplaced it's beat. Most of us have learned a dance of sorts within the narrow perimeters of a small exacting square that encloses. If we just knew how to knock down the square's walls or open the channel of our heart's rhythm, or open to our inner voice we would be free. We would begin a movement so beautiful, so fluid, so perfect that our souls would twirl. And, in our hearts we *know* that to be truth.

In our dreams, we move most magnificently in the splendid fluidity of Divine motion. In our waking reality, we stumble sleepwalking through the very illusions we created. Alas, many even opt to sit this one out. It is a choice. We could choose to begin now. If we are willing to risk breaking out of our boxes of limitation and discover the ancient tribal gyration that is encoded in our spirits, we *can* begin. We can embark on an ancient trail leading to the origins of earth-based spirituality that will re-kindle the flame of dance within. As the stirring inside spills out and overtakes our exteriors, we *will* hear the whispered invitation to ceremonially release, restore, renew, and re-craft our lives as spiritual dancers. I chose to dance.

That dance began, for me, in New Mexico with a warm-hearted Toltec Nagual, an impassioned Mestizo healer, and a crazily wise Druid/Cherokee couple who bore an uncanny resemblance to Roseanne Barr and John Goodman. When I met this trio (individually not collectively), I was locked in a castle with no long braid for rescue and involuted muteness that had rendered my notes imperceptible. Today, I can whirl in front of people, *and do*. My voice, though soft in pitch, *is* heard and its music requested by an audience more public than I would ever have imagined.

You *too* can become an artful dancer in your waking life. Allow me to take your hand and walk with you onto the magical dance floor of Shamanic practice as I share my story and awakening. For it is here, that I acquired both a rhythmic left *and* right foot and a trance of motion that catapulted me to magical realms, then stepped prancing them down into my everyday life.

This is the story of how I found my way to a life worth living. I entered the circle of the medicine wheel and learning to align myself with that which is natural as averse to that which is culturally imposed as domestication. It is ultimately a tale of my transformation out of the mundane Tonal life to experiencing a personal ascension into a life of Nagual magic.

Some of my story may seem a bit fantastic or phantasmagorical. As a left-brained, rational person at the time, the events that unfolded turned my world upside down, inside out, and shook me up in ways that I could not have fathomed.

All I can say to the reader, is the events happened. You will process them within the constructs of your reality. If you are prepared to stretch your former boundaries of solidity a bit; you may find yourself as much in awe, as I did in those years of magic unfolding.

And, ultimately, I hope you will discover that we are all dancing to a whispered voice if we just listen.

DEDICATIONS

My story is dedicated to the teachers I encountered who moved me onto the shamanic path. It is also dedicated to all the wonderful metaphysicians that graced my life during the period. I am also *so* aware of the magical lands that I was drawn to whose electric energy moved me into an exploration of senses and experiences far beyond the norm.

A special tribute to my youngest son who has honored this work that I do and asked me to teach his son some of the magic of the path. To the ancestral DNA which I carry that helped me absorb and incorporate these teachings and experiences with minimal questioning and doubt.

And, finally for the Ancient Ones whose thoughts, stories, and wisdom has come to me in downloads at times when I most needed to understand and accept a path that was most definitely lesser traveled in this timeframe.

I have been most blessed by a life more magical than I could ever imagine. As Maya Angelou said, I've carried rainbows in my pockets. Hopefully I shared that magic with people in ways that helped them open corridors of wondrous discovery.

CHAPTER I.
STRANGE HAPPENINGS

Owl Woman

Holy Spirit Visitations

I'd gone to bed with a black eye mask and earplugs as part of a sensory deprivation meditation practice. Suddenly I became acutely aware that there was a presence in the room; it was palpable. My heart raced, thumping in my chest as fear started to take over. Grasping ahold of reason, I asked myself *"was anything bad happening?"*

Realizing that nothing untoward was indeed occurring, I began to relax. I felt some movement about me but no overt actions that in anyway made physical contact with me. Deciding to just relax into whatever was happening, I simply allowed myself to feel the energy about me.

Later, I would refer to this occurrence as a visitation by what I dubbed *"The Holy Spirit."* It happened in other meditations as my work with the studies of The Nature of the Soul continued.

Seattle and Nature of the Soul

The first inklings that my life was to dramatically change, happened in Seattle, Washington. After years of being agnostic and then starting to explore religions to see if any fit, I also explored other bodies of knowledge. The Course in Miracles was one. I found it useful to a point, over the years, though observed that many who carried it around like a bible were still unhappy in their lives. Perhaps more impactful, for me, was The Nature of the Soul which was introduced to me in the greater Puget Sound area.

Even slightly before that exposure were three visitors at Unity Church in Seattle. A lovely woman, Asha Pravor, came to the church to talk about her involvement in the Ananda Community in Palo Alto, California and her guru.

She related a story of the elder guru being asked to give a talk at an important anniversary. The guru was carefully brought before the devotees. Smiling, yet frail perhaps from an illness, he looked out over the crowd and said merely three words: *"God, God, God."*

It was the way she told it and the way those simple three words were shared that caused a chill to run through me. Somehow, I'd attuned to that event and the proclamation of her guru. An indefinable quark, if you will, opened in my cosmos of spiritual awakening.

Next came Marianne Williamson, before all her fame. She was hip, happening and attractive. That, however, was just the veneer. What occurred for me in listening to her story was the first palpable feeling of, that heretofore illusive quality, faith. I could feel the faith that she spoke of whereas it had merely been a concept before.

Lastly David Spangler visited speaking to the topic, manifestation. For the second time this word faith came up. His devotion to what he was sharing, and talk, had again evoked that chill through my body feeling that I later came to understand as spiritual affirmation.

When my good friend, Elizabeth, invited me to explore The Nature of the Soul with her, I was ready. Greg was our teacher, and a kinder, dearer, gentler soul I'd not yet met.

Some of what happened, as I worked with the Nature of the Soul material, may have been attributed to the setting, the teacher, the nature of the offering and a void in my life that needed filling.

Having been self-destructive to the point of suicide since teens, when I decided to give up the Drama Queen role, there was an opening in my life. As all vacuums seek to be filled, spiritual discoveries began to unfold for me as I surrendered the past.

Nature of the Soul studies had sufficient mental challenge to engage me while offering longed for spiritual succor. As a channeled body of work, it was devoid of religiosity yet, somehow embodied some of the best of the teachings of mystics and masters of record.

I found, as I engaged the material and practiced the exercises, that many things began to shift for me. Often as Greg spoke to experiences we might be having; I'd share what my personal ones had been. At times, I thought I must be doing something wrong as my experiences were not what he'd suggested. As it turned out, he often said, I was ahead of the material.

My meditation practices took an unexpected turn also. I'd not meditated before though now engaged in earnest. The *"Holy Spirit"* experience that I shared above, became increasingly the norm. Whether I was practicing sensory deprivation at night or sitting in the day, I often felt a presence was with me. It became more comfortable to live with this unidentified essence around me without need to know more about who or what it was.

Sometime during the Nature of the Soul studies, I experienced another phenomenon. I later thought of this as experiencing angels in human bodies.

On or around my birthday in 1989, a friend handed me an airline ticket to New Mexico. My home had been decorated in a Southwest motif for decades, no matter where I lived. I was often heard to say that one day when I was famous and rich, I'd move to New Mexico. My friend apparently got the message that the time was now.

I'd always been called to Santa Fe since visiting it probably in the late 60's or 70's. I assumed that was where I was headed on the visit. There I went first on arrival in the Land of Enchantment. Surprise, it was visually as I remembered, save the old western diagonal parking, but didn't seem to be inviting me.

People I encountered, as I was exploring and made that knowledge public, were very discouraging. They said everyone was working multiple jobs and costs were high. It felt snobbish and fake. Truly, I was taken aback as I'd expected it to be wonderful.

Back to Albuquerque and viva la difference. There people were welcoming almost to a fault. When I announced my intention to move there, the welcome (*Bien Venidos*) rugs were rolled out effortlessly.

Contacting the woman who headed up a department in the state government, I was immediately invited out to dinner. Everything seemed to support my moving, to Albuquerque.

I returned home and announced my intentions to move. It was heady and scary, the choice, all at once. Never in my life had I not made a move that was either determined by a male prerogative-father, husband, lover etc. This was a first.

Joseph's Angelic Presence

Preparing to move, I put a large object up for sale. That was the point at which Joseph, aka angel in human embodiment, came into my life. I'd advertised a large, cumbersome piece of exercise equipment in the local paper. Had several calls inquiring and then someone who called Joseph phoned. He wanted to buy the piece but couldn't come until after 4:00 pm.

I was most hesitant to keep it for him, not knowing if he would indeed show up or not. He assured me that he would absolutely come for the item. Somehow, I trusted him.

My youngest son and I were living together in the Green Lake area of Seattle at the time when Joseph showed up at our door.

He was a nice looking, gentle appearing man with whom we immediately felt comfortable. I showed him the equipment in my office. Joseph began to ask my son, and I, questions and spoke to us as if he'd known us forever. There was an unexplained comfort level with him. As he talked with us, he also seemed to know things about us that he could not possibly have known.

Time simply suspended as we spoke with him. Dinner time came up and I invited Joseph to stay and eat with us. He accepted.

During dinner, he asked me if I'd read *Siddhartha*. I had not. He suggested that I get a copy and read it. He spoke of some mundane things like his family and wife, but mostly talked of things spiritual. The ease and comfort of having this man in our home and life was amazing.

The sun was setting as he left us with warm hugs for both of us and promises to get together again. We both stood on the porch watching him go. After he left, we both expressed how much we would miss this total stranger. Intuitively we knew something profound had happened.

Sometime later I tried to contact him as there was such a strong call to connected with him again; almost a deep yearning. The numbers he'd provided us with simply didn't exist. Thus, began my perception that not all things that occur in the material world are in fact material. Joseph's appearance began a profound period of magic and discovery.

The magical experience with Joseph, the Nature of the Soul material, and the three guests at Unity served to turn my life in a completely new direction. The world of that which is spiritual, paved the way for my major transition as I headed to mystical New Mexico.

I chose to leave Seattle on March 8th, International Women's Day, as that day had marked the ending of my first marriage and the beginning of adult emancipation for me. It was my intention to be set free!

CHAPTER II.
MAGICAL MOVE

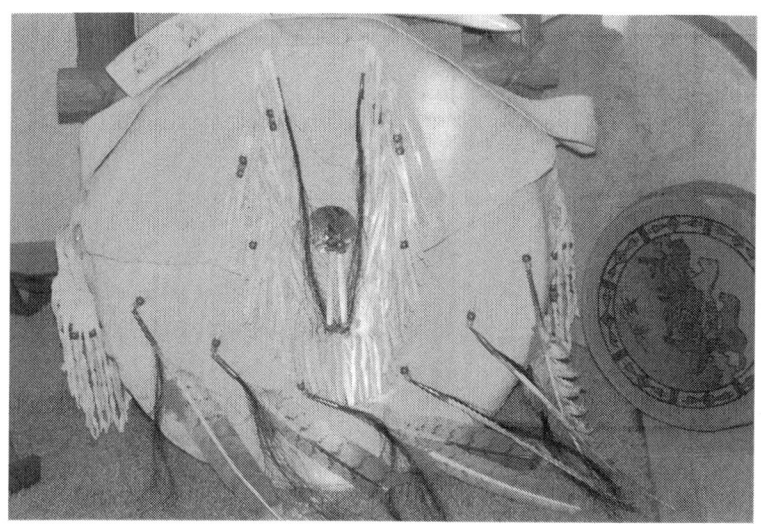

Drum Case by Student Gerald Whitehawk

Magical Call and Magical Move

Everything was almost dreamlike about my move to New Mexico. My friend Jonell and I drove the U-Haul truck from Seattle to Albuquerque. Snow storms were all about us except for the actual patch of highway we were on. Seriously, some corridor opened the road ahead and we drove in perfect safety amidst storms swirling all about the sides of the same byway.

We had so much fun being gal truckers and singing *"On the Road Again"* with Willie all the way. Two short stops from Seattle and we arrived. I put Jonell on the airplane back to Seattle and began my relocation.

People said it would be challenging to find good, affordable housing. Voila! I found a beautiful casita in a complex (Los Terrones) with authentic Mexican/Spanish décor in the North Valley area bordering on Corrales and near the Rio Grande. Saltillo floors and Mexican tile accents abounded. My first greeter was a neighbor offering Amish Friendship bread. The truck was unpacked and I was settled in three days.

Next, I'd been warned that it would be almost impossible to find a job that paid anything near the scale of Seattle. Within the first month, I found a position in nearby Bernalillo that paid even more than what I'd been earning in the Pacific Northwest.

Within the first weeks, my boss who'd painted the building purple in a man's industry, invited me to meet her psychic and spiritual group near the Sandia Mountains. Thus, began a period of my life that was so unimaginable to a left-brained accounting type that I find it may be challenging to convey. I can only tell you how it all unfolded though I understand it may not make sense to you the reader. However, I will do my best.

The magical qualities of New Mexico at that time were almost palpable. With the Sandia's, the river, high desert, and a vast canopy of stars at night, including the constellation Orion over my door, how could it be anything else? Population was, at that time, not so overwhelming as to disrupt the natural energies. Perhaps it was the ideal time to be there.

Aurora

Aurora, was the psychic that my boss recommended to me. My Seattle experiences were about to be exponentially outdone in in her presence and my life would never be the same again. She had an energy that opened the mystical in my life. A wave of the arm and a trail of light and energy followed.

As I began to attend Aurora's weekly soirees and then worked with her individually, a shift happened. There was many a night driving home, from the Sandia's to Los Ranchos, that all the lights went out on my car. It was common for me to drive home in the dark. Other nights the panel worked fine just not on the Aurora nights.

When I walked at night near street lights, they began to go out as I passed by; returning to on, after I was well away from them. If I touched a water faucet it dripped. I even shut down the computer at work by simply touching it.

Fortunately, my boss was not off put and remarked, *"you have a strong electro-magnetic field."* I subsequently learned to ground myself before touching anything that had an electric current.

It was during this period that I also began to see some people like paper cut-outs against whatever background or landscape we were in. This was mostly with people who were very spiritual and, for me, it made real that concept that this life is a dream we are having. It isn't anywhere near as concrete as we imagine.

Aurora's past-life regressions with me helped explain a lot about my present life. I'd always felt my step-father, mother and I were in some competitive, triangular relationship. As it turned out we'd been doing that dance for many, many lifetimes.

My step-father and I were twins in another lifetime during the period of the major influence of Genghis Khan. My mother came between us and one of us killed the other. As the other lifetimes played out, I could easily see the power struggle, jealousies, and competition for affection unfolding. In all the lifetimes after the first, they'd killed me.

Understanding that, I decided right then and there, the gig was up; no more. I laughingly announced this to them as a declaration: *"I'm not going around with you two again."* Of course, they were completely mystified as to what I meant yet I knew, in the deep place of knowing, that the message was received.

The Aurora period lead to the beginnings of feeling healing power in my hands. I was with a male friend one night. In a discussion about his life he'd become highly agitated with rising anger. Instinctively, I put my hands on his solar plexus as he ranted. My hands began to feel hot. After just a few minutes he suddenly became very calm and stated that something had changed in him. He'd completely lost his anger and visually changed. We never spoke about what had happened specifically; though I knew something had.

This many years removed, it is challenging for me to know the exact unfolding of all the events. I know I attended workshops and classes on almost any topic relating to metaphysics and spirituality.

E'Star and Jessie

Perhaps I saw an advertisement of Garthenia E'Star and Jessie's mask making workshop; perhaps someone told me about it. The event was held in the South Valley of Albuquerque. If people were concerned about my safety living in the North Valley, they were almost ballistic when I announced I was venturing into the South Valley. Venture I did.

My best description of Garthenia E'Star and Jessie was an impression of Rosanne Barr and John Goodman. Their house was unorganized and messy; not the cleanest place I'd ever been either. To say I found them unrefined would be an understatement. Yet, there was something compelling about these two characters.

Our first workshop together was shamanic mask making. The crowd was as diverse as our hosts and the neighborhood they lived in. Garthenia was part Cherokee and they both embraced the Celtic path of earth-based spirituality.

We journeyed, my first time, for a vision for our mask. Working in pairs; one built the mask on their partner then the reverse. What particularly struck me after my mask was removed in plaster relief, was how powerful my face looked. I saw what others had seen for years and I'd not recognized. If you've ever had a mask made on your face, you too may have an impression that changes your self-perception as you see yourself in relief.

Working with a partner we looked at the top of the face, the bottom of the face, the left side, the right side and overall. Each was a study in persona and we exchanged impressions of the mask we'd built to the recipient. We also observed how the masculine and feminine side of our faces are quite different; something more apparent in plaster relief.

There is a huge healing that can take place in mask making. What I observed over many years, is that when the mask is on each person before it is removed, their features are just perfect. In the flesh, a person may not like this or that feature, yet in plaster relief there is a beauty that comes through.

My other observation was that when you are building the mask, it is complete and you step back to observe it as it dries on your partner you can get an overwhelming feeling of being The Creator. You've a sense of perfection and grace that is hard to properly language.

After that workshop, I came to a shield making workshop; another first. My journey for a vision on this one showed me that I was being given a long golden rod with a crystal on the top. Simple yet amazingly powerful.

One child in attendance wondered why my shield was so simple. However, I got the message loud and clear. I was to be a wayshower for people; a guiding light.

Soon after the first workshops, Garthenia and Jessie invited me to attend their one year Celtic Shamanism class. Thus, for a year I drove to the South Valley and learned about energy, magic, visions, journeying. In one of the workshops I saw auras for the first time around the couple. Theirs just popped out and I experienced the wonder of seeing.

In addition to classes, they hosted a monthly sweat lodge and kiva ceremony; both had been built in their backyard. Not a fan of heat I was a bit freaked about being in the lodge. They were so gentle with me and let me be an antler person which is the coolest of the hot places in a sweat lodge. As a bonus, you could slip your arm through the blankets and touch air if you needed to feel more secure.

I learned to work with fire through the lodges and loved all the wonderful ceremonies we held in the kiva including celebrating Samhain. At that special time, we opened the Sipapu in the middle of the Kiva and placed very small objects of loved ones that had passed in the year prior. A peace pipe was passed and that ceremony shared.

Over time I came to truly appreciate Garthenia and Jessie for all the amazing things they shared, believed in, and served as example to seekers. The condition of the house faded into oblivion as gratitude for their offerings became much more important.

Between Aurora's offerings, and Garthenia and Jessie's, along with many other workshops, I moved comfortably into an earth-based appreciation and embraced the teachings. Unity Church and Church of Religious Science also became refuge places for me and offered other metaphysical teachings and discovery.

That was the first year of living in the Land of Enchantment and it certainly lived up to the name. The energies at that time were so powerful that I feel any serious seeker would have experienced awakenings.

I came to understand the sacredness of all land and so appreciated the basic precepts of ancient wisdom.

CHAPTER III.
OTHER WORLDS

My heritage clock Celtic and Mongolian

Magical Watch Band

As I had been exposed to new energies and had begun to experience more, another bit of magic occurred. There was the watch band story; a memory early on of the mystical occurrences that became common place during my epic spiritual odyssey that was New Mexico.

One day I was attracted to items in the window of a Native American goods shop in Old Town Albuquerque. Of interest was a Native American beaded watch-band. At the time, I was wearing a watch with a metal band that was not working. The battery had died some time ago.

Looking at the watchband, it appeared that my current defective watch face would fit it. I asked the clerk to load my watch onto the beaded band. Haplessly, I set the watch to the proper time, as if it would run.

Hours later after leaving the store with my gorgeous new band, I glanced at the watch head. Amazingly it had kept perfect time. I wore it for the rest of the day and it stayed right on time. Took it off that night and placed it on my night stand.

The next morning, I picked it up and it had again stopped. Curious, I set it again and put it on. Same phenomena, it ran the whole day. Off at night, it stopped; on during my active day; it ran.

This saga of the watch continued for several years with one odd exception. At any time that I was visiting one of the pueblos for ceremony or conducting an important shamanic ceremony, the watch quit running during the ceremony; time simply suspended.

Speaking of bands, there was another type of band or bond that occurred during this period. I built friendships with people I'd met through Religious Science. One of my friends and I were having lunch one day. As we shared, we touched on phenomenal experiences that we'd been having. We felt safe enough to disclose them to one another.

As the conversation went on, we concluded that there were probably a lot of people who'd had such experiences and never shared them. We decided to host an event at her home inviting anyone who was willing to be open and share the fantastic with us.

50 people showed up! Truly it was beyond our wildest dreams. As we went around the circle, each person came out of the closet telling us what phenomenal thing had happened to them that made them feel set apart. I'm sure it was very healing for everyone just to know that here was a safe environment for such a revelation.

A couple of people came who seemed to be more fundamental in their spiritual/religious orientation. I have a vague memory of some bit of discord with that though we managed it and they too, shared their stories.

Miguel and Mother Sarita

One important thing that came out of the event for me personally, was meeting Elena Avila. It turns out, she and I had had a mutual man friend/lover; not at the same time.

He thought we'd get along famously and we sure did. We were both a little wild and crazy and practicing spirituality that was not in favor with the norm at the time.

At the time, Elena was studying with Don Miguel Ruiz along with practicing Curanderismo. She introduced me to Miguel at his birthday party. While I was a fun person; I was not a party girl. There was a lot of hesitancy on my part attending. For one thing, I'd be one of the few non-Hispanic people there.

That said, it turned out to be a fortuitous meeting. Miguel, small, warm and with penetrating eyes announced to me that night, *"You will study with me!"* I believe my response was something like, *"really?"* I didn't know him and wasn't sure I wanted to commute to Santa Fe along with that white thing.

Yet commute I did, up La Bajada in all weather conditions. Miguel's group met in circle at Gaia's home in Santa Fe. Always there was prayer and a parable. Much like the simple teachings of Yeshua Ben Joseph, Miguel favored the parable style of teaching. He was adept a creating an environment of love and acceptance for all the diverse group in attendance.

At one point, I invited my friend Simran to join us in group. It was not long until Miguel approached us and informed the two of us that we would apprentice with him. My response was as before, *"really?"*

Somewhere in the teachings, Miguel gave a demonstration at a Santa Fe library in which he explained the physical, etheric and soul bodies that we each have. That struck me as a more definitive class than many of the story telling times at Gaia's.

In an individual session with Miguel he informed me that I was a "Nagual" (magician/teacher/shapeshifter) and he was only in my life to remind me. During that session, his very dark brown eyes turned a deep blue which affirmed my impressions of his magical abilities.

We were introduced to his mother, Sarita, at one session. She was renowned as a Curandera in the San Diego area. She taught us the Egg Cleansing (Limpia) method used by Curandera's. After each cleansing, she read the person's egg not unlike tea leaf readings.

Sarita told me I would be talking before thousands of people in the future. We could say that doubt, on my part, was a factor until years later I gave a talk before 22,000 people in Japan.

Miguel gave individual apprentices assignments. Two given to me, strike me as interesting. The first was that I was to get out of my left brain for six months. At the time, I was doing a lot of accounting and a bit of marketing. The latter was my love; the former my bread.

I dropped all accounting work for the time and built up the marketing practice. It also helped to get my hands in dirt and connect with the earth. My little patch of flowers in front of my casita had major attention and nurturance during that period.

The exercise was so successful that at the end of six months, I was not editing my speech or thinking so very much. To prove the exercise had benefits, I received a call from a former accounting client with an urgent need for my services. At the job, I discovered that my left brain had simply taken flight and was not operational. Shock set in as I implored the Gods to give it back.

For three days, I moved piles of paper around and organized as I implored Spirit to restore my left-brain functionality. Finally, at the end of the third day, it kicked in! What a relief and yet how very amazing that this magic worked.

The other exercise was given to both Simran and me. I suspect that Miguel imagined that we'd had rich sex lives and several partners. He told us to make a list of all the people we'd ever had sex with before we performed an 'inventory' style recapitulation in the nude.

The night he gave us the assignment, we drove home debating just what act or acts were construed as sex acts. In retrospect, I guess we were having a Bill Clinton moment!

After we assembled our lists which were amazingly about the same length, we got together and stood naked before a mirror at my home, performing the inventory style of a recapitulation exercise between gales of laughter.

This reminds me that recapitulation was another tool we'd been given as we studied with Miguel. This type of recapitulation was called fluid. Gaia helped with those sessions. We met at Diane's home in Albuquerque for one of them. Gaia had us put ourselves in a spoke-like configuration with heads touching as we began the exercise.

Going out of body has never been a challenge for me. What surprised me was that I did not enter my own memory banks rather entered another woman's in the circle. After as we revealed our experiences and I share my weird phenomenon, Gaia commented, *"The Walk-in went farther out."* Perhaps that was the first time I'd heard that expression.

It got even more amazing that night. Sometime during the night, I awakened and realized I was not in my own body. It felt different. I realized that I'd taken on Diane's lengthier and thin body and shorter hair. It was quite an amazing experience.

The next day I called Diane and asked her if anything unusual had happened to her the previous night. I didn't give her details, initially. She told me that when she was just going to bed, she felt a presence in the room. A bit fatigued from the evening, she just said, *"do with me whatever you want, I'm tired."* When I shared with her the experience I'd had, her comment was, *"did we have fun?"* That became my first experience in automatic shapeshifting and left quite the impression.

Teleportation and Gaia

Around the same time as we were working with recapitulation, both Miguel and Gaia showed up in my bedroom at night. They sat on the bed and talked with me as if their presence was not unusual. It all seemed very real and yet often stretched my beliefs. It was certainly magical as I knew in material time that this was not possible. I cannot now remember if we ever talked about it. It was a 'just is' occurrence in that time of working with the two of them.

Elena and the Dance of the Curandera's

Abiquiu New Mexico and Ghost Ranch, on the lands that Georgia O'Keefe captured so beautifully in her paintings, was the setting for an experience that awakened me to the beauty of other traditions of ceremony and ritual.

I found myself, once again, quite the minority in the group. Many of the women were practiced Curandera's who'd studied with Elena and/or had the gift from their families. We were assigned roommates for the weekend. I remember not much caring for mine-mismatch I thought from the beginning.

Over the three days or so, the ceremonial room was thick with burning Copal and Spanish language chanted invocations. Ceremonies prevailed throughout the weekend and I was taken with just how comfortable and familiar they felt to me. The copal brought back church memories with my cousins at high mass with the burning of frankincense. It seemed to shift people out of ordinary states of being.

We were given evocative exercises to retrieve lost pieces of our souls and provoked to come out of our heads and into our hearts. At first this was a huge challenge for me, yet after the days of it, I came clean with my 'stuff.' The

Curandera's then called me Mariposa and embraced me including my roommate.

The most impactful event for me was the all-night drumming and dancing under the Full Moon in Scorpio. Time simply stopped and the dimension of material dissolved as we drummed and danced to oblivion. People took on different shapes and appearances as we effortlessly kept the beat going through the night. Magic was afoot.

I learned the Curandera greeting from the seasoned students and healers present. To this day, I teach that in some circumstances and remember its significance in connecting a circle of powerful women healers.

Ghost ranch is an amazing place to move between the dimensions and see through the eyes of both artist and healer. Elena and I cemented our long relationship with that sharing and became sisters of the heart.

Taos Pueblo

Another fantastic experience of mine in New Mexico had to do with Taos Pueblo. It had always been a favorite of mine from visiting it many years prior. I had a routine in terms of my meanderings when I entered the pueblo and visited the shops and merchants.

I'd been at the Santa Fe Opera under the stars one night experiencing a presentation that was far too avant-garde for my tastes with a friend from Santa Fe. As I looked up at the sky, a window appeared almost like a television in the sky. What I saw depicted a story of me, from another lifetime, as a Kiowa woman who'd been captured by Apaches and left at Taos for some reason.

In the scene before me, one of the Taos Pueblo men had taken an interest in me; this was forbidden under the terms of the Apache captors. There was some disagreement going on between that man and an elder.

The whole scene was like watching a drama unfolding, yet it became clear to me that there seemed to be some karmic debt being shown. I was wowed by the whole experience but never shared it with my date; returning to the opera as if nothing had happened.

Sometime later, I was to travel to Taos Pueblo with friends for a holiday. The friends all cancelled at the last minute. I decided to go anyway. About half way to the pueblo, I began sobbing spontaneously yet in some degree of joy.

When I reached the pueblo, for reasons I may never know the truth of, I decided to head left instead of right, my usual route. I wandered into a shop I'd not visited before. Always being respectful, I carefully wiped my feet before entering and then quietly looked around.

The owner came into view and I almost held my breath. He looked exactly like a modern version of the Taos man in the opera vision. Our eyes locked for a moment of some recognition. What followed was a most comfortable engagement and an invitation to become more involved with him at a business level and later, personal. Suffice it to say it was a demonstration of more magic in New Mexico.

CHAPTER IV.
THE PHANTASMAGORICAL PERIOD

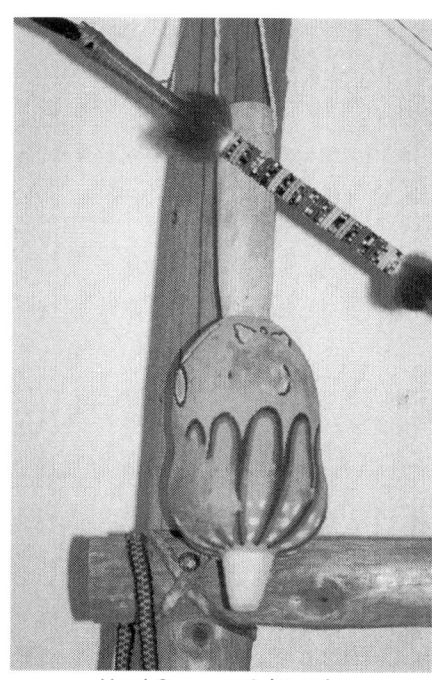

Hopi Ceremonial Rattle

11:11 Stargate

I'm not sure that anyone who has not had fantastic experiences can even fathom the next period of my life.

I'd connected and befriended other metaphysical people by this time and was involved in more than Miguel's group. There was a buzz about life as it took on more and more blending of edges in which material and ethereal overlapped.

Moving from the first casita, I was now in a condo on the same property. My youngest son had gone to his father's in Canada and I had much more time on my hands. For a short time, I had an emotional train wreck of a roommate. Thankfully that lasted only three months.

Out of that contact, however, came a connection with Norma Milanovich author of *We the Arcturians*. Norma had been a college professor and certainly not, on appearance, anyone would have suspected was having other-world contact. I met her for lunch and we immediately connected. She was involved with the 11:11 movement that Solara founded and something in her talk about it, rang true. I'd been seeing 11:11's on digital readouts for some time.

Norma was channeling Kuthumi, an ascended master who embodied the Christos energy, at that time. I decided to have her do a reading for me. During the reading, she said, *"Kuthumi wants to speak with you directly."* I was being a bit sacrosanct and flippant as he engaged me and asked,

"OK, so just which planet am I from?" His reply took me

quite by surprise. He said, *"You are not even from this Universe. If I told you the name of the planet it would not register in this reality. You are from the 3rd Universe."*

Wow, talk about being blown back! He went on to extract a promise from me about a future in teaching. There was a symbol that was to be presented to me when I'd fulfilled my promise. It was a sapphire.

As an aside several years later a fellow minister's wife painted a soul portrait if me with a blue sapphire in the middle. Additionally, my mother gave me a blue sapphire ring she'd gotten in China. I had made good my promise.

But I digress. After the reading, I called my very best friend in the world, Jonell and said, *"Hey, it's no wonder I can't find my peer group, I'm not even from this Universe."* We had a good throaty laugh.

I began to read Solara's work on the 11:11 and watched a video of a ceremony in Egypt. It moved me so much that I found myself weeping and sensed that it was an energy that I was to connect with.

For folks who haven't a clue as to what I mean by the 11:11, it was a gateway to an expansion in spiritual growth and awareness on the planet. The 11:11 commenced on January 11, 1992 (11th day at 11:11=Master Number 33) and was to end on December 21, 2012 (end of the then current Mayan Calendar Cycle).

A facilitator and group were to host the ceremony in Albuquerque. At almost the last minute, they all took off for Crestone, Colorado. My friend David and I decided to host the ceremony at his apartment's community room. One ceremony was at 11:11 am and one at 4:11 pm. We gathered about a half hour earlier to begin and give instructions. A lovely group of our friends showed up.

By mysterious synchronicity, we began the ceremony at exactly 11:11 and 4:11 on David's watch. The spiral we formed and toning was so moving. At times, it reminded me of the music towards the end of Close Encounters of the Third Kind as they used musical notes to connect. At the close of the afternoon ceremony, large, white puffy snowflakes began to fall and the landscape soon looked like a dance of white magic.

Just prior to the ceremony, I'd been reading Solara's book before I fell asleep. The copy said that we all have an angelic name. As I blew out my candles and settled down on my pillow, voices on both sides of my head started chanting, *"Amari, Amari, Amari"* repeatedly until I finally said, *"I heard you!"* From then on, my birth name was surrendered to the name I would carry forward. This is not unlike tribal renaming when one goes on their Vision Quest.

Twelve Entities

Magic then increased repeatedly as the year 1992 commenced. It was shortly after, that my intriguing twelve visitors came to live with me. Again, your belief in this may be stretched. I can only share with you my experience and assure you I was not crazy-perhaps mad-but not certifiable.

It happened one night as I finished reading an inspirational piece and blew out my candles. I was startled as it felt like six people sat down on either side of me on the bed. At first I was frozen as it was VERY real. Somehow pushing my fear aside, my curiosity got the best of me.

For the next approximate two years, these entities came to me every night. I was lifted and carried off to a place where metaphysical books were being downloaded in my head. Often when they brought me back, they'd lock hands under me and rock me to sleep.

It got to the point that I would just say, *"hi guys"* when I walked into the room but did not want to see them as I truly felt they were not human. An owl lived outside my window during this whole magical corridor and I often heard it hooting its approval.

When they very first arrived, I called my friend Garth to tell him about their appearance. I trusted his ability, at that time, to discern whether their energies were positive. He and a friend came over and spent some time in my bedroom. Exiting they informed me that not only were the energies not malevolent; they were magnificent.

I came to love this time and the travels. Occasionally I'd have to beg off for night so I could get a good night's rest. Their rocking me at the end of the nightly travels was so wonderful that to this very day I miss it though understood their work with me was complete.

Calling Animals and Bionic Woman

As the goose-bump rushes of my life grew and grew, I entered a period of more physical magic. Horses were a big part of this time. I'd long walked the dirt roads of Los Ranchos in the morning and befriended a horse called Tequila. I stopped often to give him grasses from the other side of the fence and lay my hand gently on his snout.

Then a curious thing happened. On the other side of the road were a couple of horses that started running to the fence as I passed one-day neighing. They galloped towards me and then nudged me until I placed my hand on their snouts. Apparently, there was an energy coming from my hands and presence that drew them to me.

Walking with friends one night in the area, the same thing happened with other horses. Every horse I passed wanted physical contact with me. Even visiting the Rio Grande Gorge outside of Taos, a horse up on a hill started neighing and neighing until my friend and I climbed up bramble bush and I placed my hand on his snout.

I'd always been a fast walker—walking an 11-minute mile. Yet one day as I was walking I started walking faster and faster in a power walk that exceeded human capabilities. At first I was just stunned; then some fear that I might hurt myself if it continued ensued. It stopped of course then.
I could only relate it to the Bionic Woman with capabilities that surpassed human potential.

Stray cats, and everyone's dogs wanted to sit on my lap whether I liked them or not. I'd visit someone and they would say their pet was extremely shy and wouldn't come out. Two minutes later, this heretofore shy animal was right in my lap. Capabilities and callings were woven into my every day existence during that two-year timespan. An animal menagerie of undomesticated animals also visited me especially during this corridor.

Elena Gallegos and Other Portals

Another magical phenomenon that occurred during this period of life in the fantastic lane, was discovering portals of energy in places not necessarily known to magical energy. One such place was Elena Gallegos Park in the Sandia Mountains near Albuquerque.

I could take people there with me, supposedly on a hike, and move them into places in the park where time and space suspended–it simply didn't exist. Anyone that was even remotely available for psychic phenomenon, would experience this with me. Dusk was the ideal time but not necessarily the required time.

As we'd move into the portal, coyotes would start howling, the light would change, the air had a different quality about it and some sense of elation or elevation would occur. People felt things they'd not felt before. I'd perform a ceremony to enhance the energies and to offer thanks for the wondrous experiences.

Another place that had such a portal then was the Petroglyph National Park. At dusk, I'd slip down below visibility and sit quietly calling in spirits and meditating. Often a swarm of little birds would start circling my head as I sat there–almost creating a halo around me. Again, coyotes would howl, as if they too knew magic was at play. I loved to go there can perform ceremony either alone or with a couple of other people.

Additionally, not far from Albuquerque were the Salinas Pueblo Missions National Monument that also held the mystic energy. I took a man there, that I'd been involved with, to one site (there are three) and he almost fell over from the energy and a form of déjà vu that was overwhelming for him as he stood within the ruin walls.

At that time in the area, magic was simply available on a level that years later, I did not experience. Perhaps rapid population expansion changes the dynamics of such places or maybe portals come and go. What I know to be true, at least for me, is that these special no time and no space places exist all over the planet though they may not be universally known or proclaimed.

Time Lapse

I had an interesting experience in Albuquerque with one of my metaphysical friends during this time. We were having dinner in a 50's style diner one night. At one point in the evening and our talking, we both realized that we'd actually gone back in time to the 50's. Everything took on a different glow about the restaurant we were in. We both remarked that if we went outside, we'd see cars of that period like '56 Chevrolet's etc. and a movie marque with a movie released in the late 50's. Sure enough, that is exactly what happened. Without any effort on our part, we'd time lapsed.

It was reminiscent of the movie *Field of Dreams* when the characters Ray Kinsella and Terence Mann go to Chisholm Minnesota in search of Doctor Archibald, "Moonlight" Graham. They discover that the 'doc' died sometime back. Yet in the twilight time of day Ray is transported back in time to encounter him. Except, that what happened to my friend and I was very real in that moment for both of us. This also marked the beginning of a capability to time travel at will and lead groups towards that experience.

Another weird occurrence with time lapse happened related to my job. I gave presentations to real estate companies to promote home inspection services. I'd gone out to a company in Rio Rancho to make a presentation one afternoon. A few weeks later, I was headed to the very same company. I could not find the company. Right address; no building. After some frustration, I came to accept that I'd time lapsed to before the building was built.

Other examples of this phenomena were in driving the freeway. At times, it felt as if all the cars in the freeway were in slow speed and I was in hyper speed. At others times, it was reversed. Much of this was surreal.

A further example of time lapsing occurred when I found myself at a stop light at a freeway underpass and could not figure out where I was. It seemed like I was in multiple cities at once. For a few moments, confusion reigned supreme until the time/space continuum of my rational brain kicked in.

Plant Medicine

I'd never experimented with plant medicine before New Mexico. In the 60's when psychedelic medicines were rampant, I knew in my heart of hearts that I would become one of the statistics–overdose or suicide. My emotional health at that time was much too fragile.

During my time with all the mystical and magical happenings, I met a priest in an alternative catholic church. He felt my spiritual path would be enhanced by experimenting with psilocybin-mushrooms. He'd had considerable experience with them and could guide me through a trip.

Though we'd carefully weighed out the correct portion for me, what wasn't considered was that I am slow to metabolize substances and that adding a bit more, loads my system to a monumental reaction.

At first nothing happened and then all hell broke loose. I had what I've termed a huge psychic break and destruction of aspects of my ego. After the peristalsis abated, things became smaller and larger and vision was very distorted.

About that time, I began to have an experience with Jesus. It was a dialog, almost a confessional, a sort of life review in which I could see and feel all the places that I had been less than stellar in my life and had caused harm. I remember sobbing for what seemed a very long time.

Then that period passed. I stood with my friend in front of a mirror and we could put our hands right through one another. We could make love without ever having physical contact. All senses were heightened to an almost overload stage.

Eventually, the drug affect abated and, as we stood outside, a chorus of coyotes howled as we drank in the very starry night. I asked what the time was remembering that he'd specifically asked me to recall the time we started.

What had seemed like hours and hours, turned out to be under two hours. After that experience, for some time, magical events continued to happen. I had to be careful stepping off a curb as the proportions were deceiving. We were in a restaurant and I'd look across the room at people sitting some ways away.

My vision would change and seemed to zoom in on the people. Then, I had such heightened hearing that I could hear every word they were saying though they were out of normal hearing range.

Another time we did mushrooms at Chaco Canyon. That time, I experienced being given a large body of information about the tribes that had once traveled there from Mexico and South America. The physical effects were not as remarkable yet the opening in consciousness and access to ancient information was remarkable. After that, my guidance told me to leave mushrooms alone as my body was not going to withstand the toxicity.

What the mushrooms had served to do, for me, was make real, at an emotional and feeling level, things that I'd gotten intellectually only in the past. They served a great purpose on my spiritual path.

My next plant medicine was the manufactured Ecstasy. I shared this with two male friends in the Sandia Mountains.

What struck me so much about that drug was that it caused a change in perception of beauty and love. On the drug, for me, everyone and everything became glowing with beauty.

All things were translucent making real the concept of illusion.

The two men became so amazingly beautiful though in material life they were not esthetically that attractive. As the love potion overtook me, I began to realize just how magical we truly are. I knew in my heart of hearts that if we so chose, we could fly up the mountain or jump down and fly. Fortunately, I did not test that out.

I'd been prepared for the let down the next day when the less loving world re-emerges. No regrets, it cemented my knowing that all is love and it was enough.

Spelunking in Private Caves

Have you ever been at the bottom of a cave in total darkness? Have you ever experienced in total darkness the sudden presence of light? I have and that experience can affect one's concept of dark and light.

I'd started dating a man from Carlsbad New Mexico. He was a geologist working with some private government agency tasked with disposing of radioactive waste. In his spare time, his long-standing hobby had been spelunking. Other than visiting the actual Carlsbad Cave and perhaps one other national monument, I'd only experienced caves on tours.

My friend had access to private lands where most others were not permitted to explore. One day we visited such a cave probably an hour or more away from Carlsbad. It is almost eerie entering a cave such as this; no artificial lights and recorded tour instructions. We put on the helmets with lights so that we could navigate the cave.

It took some time for us to get deep into the cave where there was no observable light. At that time, we found some rocks we could sit on and turned off our lights. The darkness and stillness was almost disturbing–something few people ever experience. As I sat there meditating, I opened my eyes. To my great surprise, it seemed that a type of light was observable. Not what we are accustomed to seeing as light–something more mystical.

My friend saw nothing as I recall yet I was very struck by the experience as just another affirmation that much of our earth experience is illusion or construct of our rational mind. The moment stayed with me for a long time.

Later, I would have another experience of light and illusion as I rode on a sunset flight from East to West coast. In each time zone that we flew through, the sun was setting. I came to accept just how very much of our experience here can be beyond our comprehension from the material perspective.

UFO's

Ugh, I can almost hear your groans! Yes, I did see UFO's during this period in New Mexico and years later in North Carolina. For those who experience sight beyond the norm, they are not so unusual. Given the clear, starry nights with an absence of artificial light and a spirit of adventure, seeing unidentified flying objects is possible.

There is a speed and type of light about them that defies illumination given off by airplanes in the night sky. I also came to feel, that when one stretches their beliefs, they appear more naturally. The very last night before I left New Mexico in 1993 heading East, after my farewell party, our entire group saw some fly above us. They seemed to be saying goodbye. I was not alone in seeing these. From what I learned from others in that time and space, many saw UFO's. And, then there is Roswell, New Mexico. You will take this for what it is worth. It was truly a sight for me.

CHAPTER V.
SIREN'S CALL SOUTHEAST: ATLANTA

Cherokee Prayer Fan

Trail of Tears

In 1993, my late friend Jonell and I came up with a rash idea about moving somewhere together and starting a business. We envisioned being a store front carrying handmade imported goods by women from countries in need of exposure and funding. We'd live happily above the store.

About the same time, my Mother asked me if I would come to Atlanta to help with my stepfather whose heart was giving out and she expected he would not last long. Mom had never been comfortable around death. I was the only one of the five children who was not attached.

Those two compelling reasons pulled me to the Southeast though my heart was very attached to the Southwest. About two weeks before I was scheduled to leave New Mexico and meet up with Jonell in Atlanta, she backed out. I understood her hesitancy as giving up her husband's financial largesse would have created a very untenable situation for her.

I'd given all my notices, said my goodbyes, and felt I was too far into the process to back out. So forward, I went. On March 8th, International Women's Day, tired as I was I loaded up the car and began the journey to Georgia.

There was an urgency about leaving on that date. It turned out to be protection for me of an oncoming major storm.

Most of the trip initially was uneventful. I got into the rhythm of the road and the miles flew by. Always for me there is a Zen moment that begins to unfold as the wheels turn on payment while I'm whizzing along on the road.

As I entered Oklahoma early one morning, I saw a sign for a local breakfast eatery. Decided to get off the exit and check it out. It was my major introduction to grits, grease and gravy which I latter observed sardonically fuels the south. An interesting experience with enough fat, protein and coffee to get me moving along into the Ozarks.

I approached the actual Ozarks at dusk. Noticing a sign to watch for deer, I slowed down a bit. In what seemed like a few moments, I saw a large stag ahead backlighted from the setting sun. He was standing magnificently in the road. There were no other cars around.

Slowing more and more, I was preparing to brake as necessary if he didn't move. He didn't. I stopped. The stag was staring at me in such a penetrating way as to be compelling. I felt overwhelmed by this stare as he walked methodically towards the front of the car.

Suddenly, he put his hoofs on the hood and then somehow thrust his head through the windshield. As he did this he turned into a bear and then an Indian man in full regalia. I began sobbing, as did he. There was instant recognition as we embraced. And, then it was over and I was still driving in the dark along the Trail of Tears. It had been a dream or journey or shift into another reality. I was stunned and elated all at the same time. Fatigue overtook me after and I stopped for the night.

The next day as I wended my way down through the Ozarks into the deep south, I kept seeing battles and blood in pictures along the sides of the road. I was somehow reliving the Civil War. I stopped in Nashville and stayed with my brother and family and then headed to Atlanta.

I arrived one day ahead of the "Storm of the Century." My brother and family had also come down from Tennessee and we were all there for the storm which shut down everything. I was so relieved that I'd heeded the urgency to leave New Mexico when I did as it was evident that I was being protected.

Universal Brotherhood and the Peace Circle

As I had connected with the 11:11 community from New Mexico, I decided to see if there were any folks located in the Atlanta Georgia area. That is how I connected with Galaya and then through her Martine. Galaya was busy traveling when we first connected via phone and she suggested that I call Martine.

Martine, also connected with the 11:11 community and the ceremony, invited me to a Peace Circle sponsored by Jeni and Rick Prigmore at their home in Duluth (outside of Atlanta).

From the first resounding greeting and hug from Rick, *"Welcome Home."* I knew I'd met people of high level spirituality, warmth, and compassion. The Wednesday evening circles became a balancing and focal point in keeping connected with my spirit each week. In rain, shine, hail, and snow, I managed to attend most circles.

There was always a ceremony and opportunity for people to talk about their paths and offerings in the community.

Often a person would be placed in the center of the circle for a group laying on of hands when healing was needed. As I learned more about the Universal Brotherhood ministry, I became aware that it represented a ministry that I could relate to and embody it's one precept, *"I hereby dedicate my life to the brotherhood of man."*

Many a night I passed a billboard on the way to Jeni and Rick's with an advertisement on it. As I returned home after the circle, the same billboard had dozens of white doves on it sans the advertisement I'd observed on the way there. I knew I'd experienced a shift in my magical attention.

During many circles, people were ordained into Universal Brotherhood. As I watched the many ordinations and listened to that very impactful ceremony, I decided to prepare for the ministry and apply. Writing my *biosketch* was eye-opening in terms of helping me identify just how much of my life and practices had led me to the decision to pursue this. I took several days up in the mountains of North Carolina to focus and draft my life experiences with religions and spirituality. I decided to dedicate my ministry to peace, making it in whatever way was presented to me.

I recalled my early impressions of ceremony with my cousins at high mass in the Catholic church. That was followed by my involvement in Rainbow Girls and Grand Cross of Color. I'd become Catholic in my first 13 years' marriage but had become disillusioned about the dogma. I was convinced that the dogma and rules had nothing whatsoever to do with the teachings of Yeshua Ben Joseph of Nazareth.

When I left the marriage, I left Catholicism. My next relationship was non-spiritual for ten years. When it was complete, I'd returned to the search I've mentioned earlier.

The words just poured out of me and I probably ended up delivering one of the more verbose bio sketches. I'd visited an ancient medicine wheel in the North Carolina mountains near the resort I was staying to write biosketch. A mystical experience there brought an eagle to me as I created a sacred circle and contemplated my spiritual journey and where it was now guiding me.

My application was received well and they found me worthy. I became ordained in late November 1993 with my mother and youngest son in attendance. A picture taken at the ordination showed a mysterious light projecting from my head to the top of the room. The service was very empowering and spurred me on in ways that unfolded as my three years in Georgia revealed.

I'd had discussion with Jeni about my prior experience of Reiki as a marketer promoting a practitioner. I told her that I just didn't feel a connection with the woman enough to have her teach and attune me. Jeni revealed that she was a Reiki Master. Voila! I'd found my teacher. An excellent teacher she was as we were so very aligned.

As the initial attunement and subsequent ones were given over 2 years, people presented themselves to me for healings. I did not have a formal practice yet had plenty of volunteer clients who came to very much tout my new skill.

During that time, I also experienced just how amazingly

powerful Reiki can be for acute situations. I'd smelled plastic burning in my dishwasher. Thinking that the cycle was done, I opened it up, rolled out the drawers, and reached in to retrieve the damaged plastic. Accidently, I touched the heat coil which was live. Jerking my finger out of the device, I saw it looked like burnt pork rind.

As tears streamed down my face, I wrapped the other hand around the burnt finger and began sending Reiki and activating the symbols repeatedly. Eventually the pain abated. I removed my hand and lo and behold, ALL the skin had returned to normal and there was just one small reddish spot. It never even blistered. Reiki was truly miraculous.

During the time of the circles, Jeni became quite ill. She asked me to facilitate the circles in her absence. I'd mentioned to active participants and friends that I'd established, that I had shamanic training in New Mexico. It was natural to bring that into my ceremonies for the circle. The ceremonies were very well received.

I came to realize that part of the true reason I'd been called to the Southeast was to become a UB Minister and to share my knowledge from New Mexico.

Kituwah Festival in Ashville North Carolina

Finding Georgia's energy to be quite dense at times, I'd often traveled to North Carolina. As I'd cross the border, some shift would happen; the air was lighter and I felt freer. Those journeys were salve for my soul especially with the heaviness of my father's protracted passing time.

I'd visited Asheville and very much loved it. Also, found the Light Institute at Black Mountain to be quite wonderful and transformative in its own way.

Friends told me about Kituwah, a festival of First Americans, healers, speakers, metaphysical books and good, etc. I was very drawn to attend. Schedules and obligations forced me to put off deciding whether I could attend or not until the last minute. I had no reservations at the event, hotels etc. As magic, had become so common place in my experience, I set off firmly in the belief that it would create everything in the weekend that I desired possible.

A few stops along the way to explore a little known archeological dig and revisit jealousies and competition between attractive women, and I was on my way. A sincere compliment rendered by a gas station attendant who had nothing to gain by it elevated my mood as I wound around the mountains of North Carolina heading towards Ashville.

I'd come towards Asheville from Hendersonville and intended to stay there but saw no vacancies so headed to Bat Cave. The word "no" blazoned on neon signs all along the way as darkness set in.

Moving on from Bat Cave I entered Chimney Rock where the last mal-functioning *vacancy* sign was limply blinking. Pulled off the road and drove up a steep drive presuming the office to be in the building at the top. Seeing that it was not, I turned around and headed back down the drive.

In the Smoky Mountain mist appeared a crone. She stood at the base of the drive and excitedly waved to me. I rolled down my window and she sprang to the side, eager to tell me of her last available room.

"I'm Elsie Stafford," she said in way of introduction. A wonderful exchange ensured. Elsie, freed by seniority of correctness and custom, asked me all about myself. Her spontaneity was refreshing. The room she had was right on the highway. I told her that I had to decline it as I was in serious need of quiet and sleep. Then I said, I'd just have to trust Spirit that another vacancy would materialize.

She quickly responded, *"I know a lady who owns a motel down the street. She has a cabin she sometimes rents out. Go tell her Elsie sent you."*

I did that. She indeed had a cabin which she even discounted for me. I ended up with an entire cabin high above the highway all to myself for the entire weekend. Serendipity continued as I had a delightful dinner experience as the only patron at a local restaurant that stayed open to accommodate me.

The next day I had a pleasant exchange at a small eatery then headed to Kituwah. The dancing began and lasted two and a half hours. This caused me to be late getting tickets for the Wisdom Keeper sessions. Undaunted when I saw the "sold out" signs, I wandered downstairs to look at arts and drafts.

Ran into a friend who asked me if I was going to the Wisdom Keeper sessions. I said I didn't know and headed over to an usher that I saw near the entrance. I told her that I wanted to go to the sessions and asked what it would take for me to go. She directed me to go upstairs and give them her name. I ended up with a front row seat and nice connection with two native women. Magic prevailed.

Working with Weather

In the south, tornadoes can and do happen. Through my shamanic training, I'd learned to bring on rain with my Amazon rain stick and a bit of a dance and intention. I had occasion in the deep south to work another aspect of weather, reversing extreme weather.

I'd been visiting a friend's house in the rural area of Atlanta and house sitting. Alarms sounded indicating a potential tornado had been spotted in the area. I sat quietly in the center of the house with a candle lit and moved myself into a deep calm. Visualizing that I was at the very center of the storm and still, I sat through the storm in perfect peace. The storm blew over without major force winds but the tornado missed the house. There was no damage.

I thought about moving clouds much earlier when I lived in Colorado and as a child laying on the grass. It reminded me of the power of our intention to affect nature. What seemed like a unique phenomenon, I was reminded, is untapped potential for managing energy.

Another time I was staying in a motel somewhere in Georgia on a trip and the television flashed a warning for tornados in the vicinity. I began to visualize the spiral of the storm. Slowly and purposefully, I started reversing the spiral, lifting the energy, and dissipating it over a broad area to cause no harm. No tornados developed that night.

Finally, and after I left Georgia, my mother called me in the middle of the night telling me a tornado was headed straight to her home. I gave her specific instructions as to where to sit in the house, which candle to light and then began work on the storm. Success! The tornado blew through but completely missed her condominium. Neighbors had some damage but none to my Mom's property.

Since that time, I've often worked on storms either alone or in concert with others (including former students) who believe in our ability to work with nature. This, for me, affirms that all things in creation are nature and we have a relationship with them as energetic beings. When we align with the elements, they work favorably with us.

Etowah Mounds

The Mississippi Mound Builders left remnants of their cultures throughout the Southeast much as the Pueblo Indians left structures in the Southwest. My curiosity was aroused as I decided to visit as many as I was able particularly in Georgia and Alabama. Etowah was my first and perhaps the most impactful.

This first mount site I explored alone; subsequent ones I often took students. As was my habit when I arrived, I first went down to the water. I sat down to meditate and ask the ancestors what had happened here and what I might do to help.

I was presented with a mist at first in my visioning and then it cleared and I could see the then village. I was shown the purpose for the mound and ceremonies that had been conducted there. I no longer remember the specifics of the community's demise. I do remember that when I later visited the visitor center they surmised or imagined what might have contributed in the descriptions with exhibits.

Towards the end of the vision, I asked again what I could do to be of assistance. The elders responded, *"Give the land back to the people."* Oh, my, I thought in a linear fashion, how can I possibly do that!

I proceeded to the mound, asked permission to ascend, and was also given permission to do a ceremony at the top. I felt connected with this land yet pondered just how I could fulfill what had been asked of me.

Later at every mound I visited, I was shown visions of the life that had been and what had happened to cause abandonment of the site.

Holistic School Teaching

It was not too long after visiting Etowah that a friend, from the Wednesday evening circle, asked me to meet a friend of his who was starting a Holistic Learning Institute. I met his friend, Kurt, and we ended up talking into the wee hours of the morning about possibilities for me assisting with his marketing. At the same time, he asked me if I'd be willing to teach a class about shamanism.

At that time in the deep South, shamanism was not exactly a household word. In fact, no one was offering anything by that name that I could find in Atlanta. I hadn't ever thought about teaching this subject and was a little concerned about coming out of the closet in a place where the word evoked some fear.

Yet, come out I did, and it was the fortuitous beginning of many years of helping give the land back to the people by teaching reverence for it and all things in the manifest world.

I sat at my computer and implored my guides: *"If you want me to teach this subject, please give me an outline."* Within minutes, I was rapidly typing out an outline. Then I asked for content. Again, almost as quickly as I'd requested help, my fingers were flying off the keys.

The first class of four sessions had an amazing attendance. People loved the work and responded well to my teaching. At the end of the fourth session, they asked: *"Is there more?"* I went back to the computer and again invoked the guides. At almost lightning speed, another outline was given to me. Extensive content followed just as quickly. By the end of that series, students again asked for more.

I began to branch out for venues and started teaching at local metaphysical bookstores which abounded at that time in Atlanta. This even lead to my being asked to do psychic readings. This required a lot of faith and belief that I could benefit someone by what was given to me by my guides to reveal. Whenever I was spot on in the reading, I was just thrilled and would say silently, *"It worked!"*

For three years of living in Atlanta, I built quiet a following and gave talks to groups on ancient wisdom and cross-cultural shamanism. Towards the end of 1995, I founded The Institute for Shamanic Synthesis to expand the work and train people in ancient wisdom practices.

My first group that completed the classes experienced another magical event in the North Georgia mountains at graduation. I'd decided to perform both a Shamanic Water Ritual and Fire Ritual as an initiation into the higher aspects of shamanic practice.

The site I chose was one that a well-known couple in Atlanta has aspired to develop into a retreat center. There was cosmic interference in the unfolding of their plan as their intention was not honorable on the former native lands.

I knew how to get back into the property and was aware that there was a natural small waterfall that suited the program plus space for a fire.

Several things happened that day. I'd taken one or two students with me and the rest were meeting us at a curio shop in the area so I could lead them to the site. At the shop, I noticed a Cloisonné pair of cobalt blue, heart-shaped earrings. I thought they'd be lovely for the ceremony, purchased them and put them on.

After we'd all gathered an arrived at the site, we prepared to descend a hill to the falls with all our gear. It had been raining lightly and the slopes were muddy. We joyfully slid down the hill to our site.

I established the circle as the students prepared for the initiation. I'd brought with me a cobalt rattle that one of the initiates had brought to me from a trip to Hungary. It had symbols of the four elements on it.

We were well into the Calling in Ceremony with me standing in the South. I began to shake the rattle when a piece flew off and a cobalt butterfly emerged. We all saw it and were awe struck. Later I saw that the piece that flew off was heart-shaped. And, of course, we all knew that there were no cobalt blue butterflies in this part of Georgia. Magic was to continue.

I performed the Water Ritual under the falls for each initiate. As each one was blessed with the sacred water, I gave them a special blessing meant only for their future journeys.

Our next challenge was building a fire with semi-wet wood and getting a blaze going. Amazingly we were successful and I donned a ceremonial mask as I began to work with the fire. To perform the Fire Ritual, I must become one with the fire so that as I thrust my hands into the flames, I am not burned. I graced the fire with oils and prayers for protection.

Each student stepped up one at a time, as I passed my hands and arms through the fire and then placed the energy of the fire upon them in key Chakra points. One student who'd heretofore had not been able to experience clairvoyance, was stunned that her third-eye opened as I place my fire hands on it.

After as we prepared our feast, we ended up in gales of laughter because our food was now a soggy mess. So being at play, we just scooped up the food with our fingers and enjoyed it. I was ever so grateful for all the good fortune that we'd experienced that magical day and the amazing butterfly representing transformation. Truly even though I was the leader, I was thrilled and awed by all that transpired for us.

Lesson in Discernment

Sometimes our life lessons come in such strong ways, we are forced to finally get the message. As a practicing minister, I was embracing the concept of extending unconditional love in whatever areas of my life I was capable of so doing. Then came a lesson which I chose to call: *"Unconditional love without discernment, can be dangerous."*

My last apprentice class in Georgia grew out of a presentation that I did at Phoenix and the Dragon. Several students came to me from that offering. Among them was one woman who on first impression was not only different, but a little strange.

That said, she really wanted to take the apprentice class and I reluctantly admitted her. At first things seemed basically OK with her other than the nagging impression of some undefined weirdness. She would often bring things to class that felt marginal for the earth-based teaching that I embraced.

As we got further into the studies, she wanted to get together with the other apprentices in a study group. I was picking up some hesitancy on the part of the others yet they too seemed to be overriding reason with compassion.

It all came to a head when I scheduled the graduation weekend in the North Georgia mountains. We'd arrived in a couple of groups. She was last with one other student. There appeared to be some tension and unhappiness with the two of them. I decided to just separate them and asked them to go into meditation to come to peace.

The fire ceremony was outdoors. I went out to start the fire while the others prepared in silence. In fact, I'd asked them all to be silent until I came to get them.

After the sacred fire was prepared, I invited them outside to the medicine circle. Each participant brought a candle for part of the ceremony, along with other accoutrements that I'd requested of them. I noticed that the woman in question had a big knot of hair over her Crown Chakra and wondered what she was thinking as they had been prepared for what was to happen.

We performed our Calling in of the Directions and I further prepared the fire with oils and intentions for safety. Each participant was asked to call in guides and state five things they were willing to give up and one thing they'd like to bring into their lives. Strangely this woman invoked red salamanders which are not at all supportive and yet I just trusted spirit to render that wish unfulfilled.

After her proclamation, the fire started to turn towards me. I kept working with it and invoking protection. Eventually, I felt it was safe enough for me to continue. In this ceremony, as I've said before, I am working with live fire.

To make myself save under this challenge I must become one with the fire so there is no separation between us. I had never had any issues with fire.

I started around the circle with the woman in question last. I'd initiated all but her into the fire and water rituals. I invited her to come to the center of the circle. I asked her to hold her candle to the side as I prepared to initiate her with fire.

I was at her third eye, as I recall, when I suddenly realized my arm was on fire. Stunned and committed to the silence vow I'd requested, the students stood dumfounded for moments. I just began calmly to pat at the fire on my sleeve and then requested water. The students came out of their shock and doused me in water.

Determining that my skin had not been burned, (though the candle had burned through 4 layers of clothing) I completed the ceremony and closed the circle for expediency. The rest of the day gets a bit blurry in my memory. I imagine I asked her to contact me saying we needed to talk. She left alone as her passenger hitched a ride with another student.

Again, I separated people so I could find the underlying cause of what happened. Apparently, she purposefully put her candle under the arm of my 100-year-old Slavic ceremonial gown. Further it came out that she had been trying to undermine me in the study groups and had threatened people if they revealed her plans to me. It also came out that she'd never taken the required Oath of Intention that all apprentices take to be part of advanced studies.

She'd been dabbling in Voodoo it seems and unbeknownst to me had arranged with a metaphysical store in Atlanta's outskirts to teach a class with my materials.

I refused to complete her graduation paperwork, drummed her out of the apprenticeship and disassociated myself from her. She begged me to complete her work and tried to argue with me that the burning was not intentional, however, after my findings, I knew it was all subterfuge. I did recommend she seek psychiatric help.

My gown appeared to be ruined in the mid-arm area. However, by some special blessings, I found a First American woman in North Carolina who restored it completely with clever weathering of fabric methods and salvaging the undamaged beaded trim. Today no one would ever know it had been burned.

I was, and am, eternally grateful for all the protection that I received from the other side and surely received the big lesson in discernment, loud and clear. Or so it seemed except perhaps for my relationships with romantic partners. Seems I had a faulty picker with the latter.

Florida

Like so many other supposed reasons for moving to a new locale, the move to Florida was no different. Ostensibly I was moving there to marry a fellow Universal Brotherhood minister. That lasted six weeks, then the real reason emerged.

I had a vision before I left that the relationship was doomed.

Yet, weighing the possibilities of a failed romantic relationship against becoming my mother's in-house slave and target of constant criticism, made Florida seem the better option.

In my experience, we often see the soul in someone during the infatuation stage; that, or an aspect of ourselves that they are reflecting to us. I saw my fiancée's soul; he wasn't in an emotional place to hold the vision of it. A tortured relationship with his parents and recently failed relationship left him incapable of being present in a real relationship beyond the initial buzz.

He did, however, give me a most precious gift. One day he took me up in his small airplane. He was an aerial photographer. As we floated along the Atlanta shoreline, the beauty of the water was almost omnipresent. Then we started to fly through a large cloud bank. I asked if I could open the window and stick my hand through the cloud. And, that is exactly what I did. How many people can say they've touched a cloud? Pure magic!

I realized rapidly the mistake in our pairing and ended the living together part of our relationship. To his credit, he told me I had more integrity than anyone he'd ever known for calling him out on what was happening in the relationship. As an aside, we remained great friends until his death.

What I *could* gift him besides integrity was the ability to reconnect with his parents, forgive them, and be at peace with them before they passed. I also helped his son by recognizing a heretofore undiagnosed hiatal hernia. I'd scanned his body and immediately became aware of an impaction of energy in the regions of the hernia along with a blending of colors that suggested a problem. I gave him a shamanic remedy along with some energetic healing. He experienced relief from all the prior symptoms within a short period of time.

As the true reason, I was in Florida emerged, I saw that Divine plan was being served. My gifts there ended up being twofold: one, becoming a Minister Director capable of ordaining people into our ministry who were unable otherwise to practice their healing professions due to laws; and the other being the need for a shamanic teacher. My student population grew. I enjoyed one class primarily made up of gay men, as one of the most fun classes I've ever taught.

Removed from the inherent male/female sexual tension, our group just had a blast being crazy with one another and sharing shamanism with gales of laughter. In one class I devoted a tune to one of the students. I'd done a psychic reading for him and one of the outcomes was his need for more respect. Asked if he was familiar with Aretha Franklin's Respect, he was not. To make up for the educational lack in this regard, at the beginning of the class, I played Respect at about 500 decimals. The whole class rocked out and after the bookstore owner said everyone wanted to sign up for my class.

Magic was still at play in Florida though denser energies often were more challenging to work with. A group of us were sharing a moon ceremony one night on the beach. We'd established a circle with candles around it. The tide was coming in. For the entire time, we were in circle sharing ritual and ceremony, water came in around the circle but never in it. When we completed and walked away, we looked back. The candles continued burning yet the water had now covered the circle.

In my short 10 months in Florida, I ended up feeling I'd done some good. Married a few people; ordained a few into the ministry; restored some souls through soul retrieval; facilitated healing; performed ceremony; and made some great friends through students that I am still in touch with today.

And, perhaps I might have stayed longer in the swamps of Florida but romance once again cooped my sanity and I was swept back to the Southwest towards a significant relationship with an old lover. Butterflies were to blame for the loss of reason; that and a dance that turned like into love.

Leaving the swamp presented some challenges, yet again, magic prevailed. I got as far as Ocala in my little Honda when the car started stalling. I'd spent about $3,000 on it in Ft. Lauderdale before leaving but apparently was hoodwinked. Deciding it was imperative that I get out of this new development, I headed to a Honda dealer.

I told the repair supervisor that I just needed to know whether the car was worth driving West or I should just give it up. He sent a grizzled and greasy repair man out to the lobby to talk with me. He assured me he'd have an answer for me. One and a half hours later he showed up again.

He said fifth gear was going, he had to circumvent the environmental feature and jerry-rig some other things. My question was could it make it to Sedona where I was headed. His response, *"It just might make it. Go easy on fifth gear."*

I got in the car, put my hands on the steering wheel and said to the car: *"Car you've been a great little car. I'd understand if you just can't make this long trip. We're headed home, though. If you feel you can make it, then let's go."*

Well, it cruised along just fine with improved performance as we continued West and climbed out of the swampy lands. In fact, I sold it when I got to Sedona informing the new owner of all that had been done and was needed. Six months later, I ran into him and asked how the car was doing. He said, *"Runs like a top. Never did any of the repairs!"*

Magic had by now become my byword.

CHAPTER VI.
RED ROCKS BECKON-SEDONA

Tom Blue Wolf & me in Ainu Ceremonial Robes in Japan

Vortices

Sedona visually is beyond description for the uninitiated. I believe this to be true for many. The most stunning approach to Sedona, in my opinion, is coming down Oak Creek Canyon from Flagstaff. As the red rock formations rise while you descend, it is enchanting.

Known for the four major vortices, Sedona, and the Village of Oak Creek, hold sometimes staggering energies. Airport Vortex with its heavy male energy almost leveled me the first time I climbed up to the top. My condominium was in a direct line with those energies which would later cause an illness.

Immediately, I visited the other three vortices and experienced their male, female and balanced energies along with the seasonal hordes of seekers. Over my ten months there, I thankfully discovered portals less impacted by the crowds. It became apparent that there were well intentioned healers and psychics there and then a whole coterie of pretenders. For the less discerning, Sedona was a great place to be hoodwinked if not careful. Remembering the James Ray sweat lodge deaths years later, I can see many were fooled by promises of wondrous illumination if one had the money for instant ascension.

One place lesser known, that I came to appreciate and do ceremony at, was Rachel's Knoll near Boynton Canyon. Off season, it was a marvelous place for night time rituals and then, perhaps not as trafficked as it is today.

Over time, I found portals of energy that were off the tourist map and took students there when we were working with the inner shields of transformation. Each of the major vortices were beneficial for working with the North, South, East and West; Air, Fire, Earth and Water.

I also made some great connections like Micki and John Baumann, my neighbors who were knowledgeable about stones, the energies of Sedona and connected with the 11:11 Gateway and Solara. In the short time of my stay, I wrote articles for several publications, held regular ceremonies, blessed homes and offices, taught earth-based spirituality classes, and performed healing. A lot was packed into the Sedona experience.

Small Demonstrations of Power

As I ponder some of the things that happened in Sedona, I am reminded of small demonstrations of the power of the energies that abound in Sedona.

I'd locked myself out of my condo on a Sunday with the management office closed. There was no one around who could help me and I had no hidden key for access. Remembering some of my training, I decided to move past the limitation of the lock and set an intention for the door to open without a key.

Voila! After a couple of tries, refocusing and reminding myself of no separation, it opened! Just as if I'd inserted the key; though I most certainly had not.

Another remembrance involved the script of the Worldwide Peace Meditation celebrated on New Year's Eve morning. In John Randolph Price's meditation, he talks about the New

Jerusalem rising. Perhaps that was implanted in my consciousness at a deep level.

Sometime later, I found myself driving up to Jerome AZ. The view of the Verde Valley from up there is spectacular. As I began the twisted incline to the top, I suddenly say a huge billboard that said, "New Jerusalem", with a golden city depicted. It just popped into view as I ascended.

I shook my head, as I was sure I'd never seen that sign before. By the time, I came down from Jerome, there was no such sign on that billboard. I was reminded that visions can be like that. I also thought of a movie that Steve Martin was in when he saw a personal message on a billboard that was solely for him. It also reminded me of time in Atlanta and the white dove billboard.

My medicine wheel atop the garage was positioned so that I saw Orion on any clear night. Many times, in ceremony the belt seemed to open as a door. I would lay down in the center of the wheel and energetically connect with the belt. It took me to many realms of imagination and visions.

Illness

At some point in my travels up and down Oak Creek Canyon to teach at Northern Arizona University, shop and visit my favorite Museum of Northern Arizona, I drank from the famous well along the creek. Everyone was filling jugs and naively, I assumed all was well with the water.

Not long after that adventure, I became extremely tired. I'd arise, shower and then go back to bed exhausted. Dragging myself to a regular doctor, she said my blood showed anemia. Fortunately, I was headed back to Atlanta for a conference and my ministerial sponsor begged me to see her alternative practitioner.

Her name escapes me, I think it was Zenia, and she had testing equipment to pick up subtle frequencies that suggested more serious health challenges. I held the rods as instructed and she ran the whole battery of tests.

At the conclusion, she informed me that while she normally might not reveal to someone on a first visit something as serious as she was seeing, she felt compelled to tell me as I would be heading back to Arizona. *"Cancer in the blood"* were the words coming out of her mouth. She immediately gave me several homeopathic remedies and asked me to purchase Beta Gold Glucan. Of course, rest and less stress was also part of the prescription.

I noticed her sense of urgency and returned home to take her suggestions seriously. A lovely friend suggested that I get a fountain for my bedroom to counteract the masculine energies of Airport Vortex which my bedroom faced.

I was clear in three months when I returned for a quick trip to Atlanta later for a retest.

So very much was packed into the ten months in Sedona. It reminds me of just how accelerated everything there was. It seemed to elevate drama and then ameliorate it just as quickly as it developed. Almost everyone I met was going through a lot of psychic, emotional and physical stuff there. Under this amazing natural backdrop, a lot of boils, blemishes and bumps were erupting.

My short time was blessed by two significant friendships with Brenda and Adam. Brenda was like my sister from another other mother; Adam a stabilizing influence for us both.

Magical Path

One thing that saved me from losing my sanity amidst all the chaos of Sedona's energies was an almost secret pathway that I discovered one day out walking. I'm not going to reveal specifically where this is, as that would certainly ruin its sanctity. Suffice to say it was very little trafficked, a true road less traveled. It became my habit to walk the trail overlooking the entire valley as I called in the four Cardinal Directions and invoked protection for the area, its inhabitants, and those near and dear to me.

I believe that I only encountered perhaps 4 other people in ten months and that was so grand. Twisted Juniper lauded at the famous vortices, abounded here without all the fervent dowsers and builders of stone effigies. It was amazingly quiet and serene; probably what Sedona looked like when the original Sedona and her family landed there.

As it has always been important to me since stepping onto this path, I've managed to find those serene places for meditation, contemplation, and ceremony away from the madding crowd. It is interesting to me in retrospect that I never took any pictures of this trail. Perhaps something inside told me to just hold it in my mind's memories with great gratitude.

It was this walk, the solitude and the non-allopathic meds that helped me overcome the blood disease and complete my purpose in being in Sedona. I also came to understand clearly in my short stay that this sacred land was never intended to be occupied. This was a true outdoor sanctuary: one visits, heals, and returns home. I do not believe that the original occupants envisioned a real estate boom. Most tribal people chose not to live in Sedona not just because of the high prices, rather to pay proper respect to the true purpose of the land.

Birth of Earth Ceremony in Japan

In January, a former apprentice student contacted me. She knew a Muskogee Creek man, Tom Blue Wolf, who was working with her troubled son. He was headed to Japan to a big ceremony that was looking for someone versed in Celtic Shamanism. At first, he'd thought of asking one of my teachers (not Celtic) though somewhat known at that time. I made the contact and his schedule was full. On impulse, perhaps, he asked me to come on the all-expenses paid journey and speak to the Celtic part of my heritage.

No one was running around any faster than me securing a passport, canceling my schedule, and readying myself to give a talk in front of thousands of people. The adventure was intriguing and there was no way I'd have said no.

I met Tom in Portland and we flew to Japan. We each spent one night in our individual postage-sized narrow rooms with the toilet practically in the tub. Then our hosts got us rapidly transported to the city where the venue for the ceremony was.

This place was luxury personified and I might have relished

it but we were informed that we had 15 minutes to write our speeches so that they could be translated into Japanese.

Oh my, the challenge of writing an impromptu speech to deliver to thousands of people. I decided to address what I called the Rainbow Bridge of belief between children of the moon and children of the sun. I mentioned briefly some Celtic myth and then led into why we had more similarities than dissimilarities.

The setting for the talk was awesome. Rows and rows of seats in an enormous auditorium plus extra rooms with video coverage. In all there were approximately 22,000 people in attendance all subscribing to the teachings of Okada and transmissions of light.

A collective belief in the lost continent of Lemuria, its sinking and scattering of tribes was the coalescing factor that brought these reincarnated tribes to Japan to celebrate the Birth of Earth Ceremony. Each of us was representing the ancestry of a lost tribe.

Tom and I stood together looking up at the balcony where the titular head of the organization was seated and would hear our presentations. That was a huge saving grace, not having to look at the sea of faces. My knees shook but my voice didn't waver.

Both of us were struck by how militaristic some of the pageantry, prior to the talks, was but allayed our concerns to be proper guests. After the ceremony, we were privileged to have a private audience with the titular head of the organization known as Oshienushisama. It was she who our talked had been directed to. Though our visit was brief, we were very honored to have had a private time. After, many people came up to touch us, as we'd been in the presence of someone they considered holy.

Our host was fabulous and saw to it that we visited other areas and tourist opportunities after the big ceremony. We saw Buddhist temples, reconstructed villages, gigantic parade floats and had a phenomenal 25 course Japanese traditional meal with the administrative head of the organization. Much of the landscape in Sendai was reminiscent of the Monterey coast of California.

We also performed a ceremonial ritual for 500 people at a smaller gathering. Neither of us had celebrated ceremony together before, yet magic prevailed and we were a huge success. An organic farmer from Northern Japan approached me after the ceremony.

He looked so much like my maternal grandfather, I was almost dumb struck. Apparently, he thought I looked a bit like some of his relations. Though not the first time people of Asian heritage have felt I too held some of that DNA, it was perhaps the most visually impactful. * He invited me to come up north with him to visit his farm and family. Our agenda did not allow for such a diversion.

We did, however, meet an Aniu shaman who brought with him traditional shamanic ritual attire. It was our privilege to wear some of it for pictures and learn about their many community projects.

I came to greatly appreciate the respect conveyed in Japan by elders yet many of the younger generations appeared to eschew these habits, I found it very nourishing; the bows. Japan was wonderful and quite beautiful on many levels.

*DNA testing a few years back confirmed my Eurasian heritage.

CHAPTER VII.
SONORAN SUNSETS & SAGUARO

Hopi Wedding Vase

Building a Practice

Leaving Sedona, I found my way to Old Pueblo. For me the four major mountain ranges of Tucson hold a very special energy of male and female in perfect balance. The Catalina's and Santa Rita's, north and south provide the feminine influence; the Rincon's and the Tucson's, east and west, are the masculine influence. Before Raytheon came to Tucson, and with its settlement a major population increase, Tucson was a wondrous place to further a career in promoting earth-based spirituality.

In my three years stay, I enjoyed offering many, many ceremonies and classes to a growing number of students. As with Sedona, I had articles published and was the subject of an article in a local metaphysical paper. My condominium on then Red Mesa Drive, was a beautiful place to share the teachings and hold sacred space.

By this time in my journey, I'd overcome any hesitancy in sharing with people that I was a shamanic practitioner. Any subterfuge or inclination to hid this very important part of my life had vanished. I was full on out of the closet even in my work life. One of my bosses and her daughter even took some of my courses.

My early morning walks in my complex, Kachina Hill, offered a chance to perform a daily Calling in of the Directions ceremony with an animal menagerie that included coyotes, a baby bobcat, quail families, an occasional roadrunner, and some distant possibilities of encountering a rattlesnake or two. Mr. Coyote and I often shared a good morning nod of acknowledgement as he crossed in front of me on the bridge over the wash.

In the neighborhood, giant Saguaro graced many a private entrance and nearby was an almost forest of these amazing standing people. I was even brave enough to hug one; ever SO gently. I came to feel that they held so much of the history of the Sonoran Desert lands, that being literally in touch would render tales of other times.

The power of these ancestors, the intensity of the desert fire and the mountains proved to be an ideal place to share the wisdom of the Good Red Road.

Agua Caliente Park

Water becomes quite an issue when one lives in the desert. While the wild life and desert flora and fauna are amazing, I came to miss water. Being introduced to Aqua Caliente Park by my friend, Tom, was a saving grace.

Among the tall palm trees and grasses of the park, there was a natural spring and ponds with ducks, turtles etc. I found a serenity at the pond in odd hours and seasons when tourism was diminished.

What was an otherworld experience, was to sneak in after dark with a group to perform ceremony. In the quiet of the night, with moonlight and no other people, this proved to be a nourishing and energetic place to drum, sing and perform shamanic rituals. The element water, during so much desert fire, served to balance out intentions and nicely invite feminine influences. I'm certain that the ghosts of indigenous ancestors who long visited what were then hot springs, contributed to the depth of our experiences there. We always left things exactly as we'd found them so as not to in any way negatively impact the park's eco system.

Sabino Canyon

Yet another water source in my early days in Tucson and site of many full moon rituals was nearby Sabino Canyon. When I was first introduced to it, water was so abundant in the canyon that it flowed over bridges atop washes and gullies. Prairie Dogs, who symbolize retreat, in Jamie Sam's Medicine Cards, were abundant at the entrance. Coyote, bears, rattlesnakes, and mountain lion were also residents, though infrequently encountered or welcomed.

My students enjoyed the feminine flow of water in the canyon much in the way Agua Caliente had complimented ceremony thorough feminine influence. There were also small caves along the trails that I later used with intensive students for recapitulation exercises.

Ceremonies under the moonlight at Sabino with a sacred circle drawn in the dirt, afforded all of us protection and an energetic that magnified our ceremonial intent. Quiet times under the stars and moon in nature I've found, are salve for any unsettling events in one's life. Many 'aha' moments were experienced by participants at these Moon Ceremonies along with an overall sense of well-being in mind, body, and spirit.

I remember one time that one of the attendees was having heebie-jeebies about the possibility of our encountering rattle snakes on the partially dark trail. Knowing that this fear might attract the very thing she was afraid of, I counseled her to either set aside her fear with trust, or leave the group so as not to compromise their safety.

Fortunately, she chose the former, not the latter, and was happily surprised that nothing untoward happened to herself of the group.

In retrospect, I feel fortunate that I had come to completely trust the sanctity of sacred circles for providing protection to all within them. Without that total trust, I would have potentially put lives at risk. Trust became increasingly an important issue as my shamanic journeys continued.

Radio Show

As I look back now the first Tucson years were so filled with activities to promote shamanic pathways, that I know there were blessings far beyond the known or quantifiable in experiencing successes.

I came to feel that a radio show in which I would interview diverse shamanic practitioners would truly promote the benefits of ancient wisdom. With the financial support of a dear friend, I could inaugurate 'Shaman Talk" through a station in Phoenix. It ultimately turned out to be more of a vanity station, gathering revenues, than one that truly supported its programs, yet it was a great venue for a short duration.

It was my great privilege to interview, Barbara Hand Clow; Brooke Medicine Eagle; Eleanora Amendolara; Christina Pratt; Tom Blue Wolf; Jaichma & Vicente Rutury (Huichol Shaman); Jo Schmidt; Elena Avila and Don Miguel Ruiz. Some of the guests were friends; others recommended to me as sources of amazing shamanic wisdom. My final show was with my teacher, Miguel, as he was becoming recognized through his book, The Four Agreements.

I learned a lot about just how much work goes into producing a radio show and interviewing. Hours were spent in preparation of their subject material, biographies, and preparing a closing meditation. It was a lovely experience and I am eternally grateful for my guests, their amazing talents and willingness to share their wisdom in a broadcast medium before technology brought us to podcasts etc. Some of the interviews were done at the studio in Phoenix; some at my home. Most were recorded though we lost a couple due to technical difficulties.

Intensives & Sanctuary Cove

My website, developed during my Sedona days, was beginning to attract attention. I decided that as I had a truly beautiful space and extra room, to offer 3-7 days' intensives for students to visit and work with me individually. This offered the possibility of absorbing more material in a one-on-one setting tailored to the student's level of understanding and needs.

One of my first guests was my dear friend, Rainer from Germany. He was very advanced in healing modalities yet wanting more exposure to cross-cultural studies and traditions. There was an instant chemistry that made working with him easy and rewarding. We ended up having two more intensives; one with his wife.

A particularly impactful experience we have was at Sanctuary Cove in West Tucson. You are probably figuring out that I like to go to sacred places in off times (i.e. when they are closed to the public). Yes, I confess, that is/was true.

Sanctuary Cove was introduced to me by my late friend, David, as a place that I might enjoy the views and energy. There is a small chapel, an outdoor amphitheater, and vast lands to explore. Explore them Rainer and I did one evening.

We visited the chapel, performed ceremony, and then climbed up to the top of the hill above the amphitheater. I instructed him to lay down and focus on a place in the heavens. Guiding him to connect with a strong etheric cord to that place, I invited him to journey for information, energy reclamation, and general discovery. He had quite a profound experience and, as we completed, the coyotes howled as they had so often done in other times and places when magic was abundant.

On the way down, we found an alraune, what could be described as a witch's divining stick in German. It was shaped, in part, like a woman with long thing arms reaching up to the sky. I had that stick for many, many years, though it one day disappeared almost as magically it had appeared.

Two other experiences I had with Rainer were taking him to Sabino Canyon for a cave Recapitulation experience and then to Colossal Cave to journey.

Other students from as far away as Kuwait and with varying religious backgrounds including Buddhists and Muslims also came during my three-year stay. My wonderful student Jalila and I traveled to Sedona where I could help her awaken her inner shields in each of the four powerful vortex locations.

In fact, it was on that journey that I received my next message of a move out of Arizona. Having trusted Spirit before, this was no exception.

CHAPTER VIII.
HEART OF TEXAS

Center of Altar

Austin Community College & Teaching

As with all of my moves since New Mexico, I'd experienced a nagging disruption in my activities and connections in Tucson. I call these the '*betweens*.' They represent a place where in all the things that were working, and working well, suddenly begin to break up and a restlessness creeps in. And, so it was with Tucson in 2001.

My youngest daughter was planning to go to the University of Texas in Austin that year. That was the beginning of the call to Austin. She'd not lived in any place as long as she'd lived in Southern California and was a bit nervous about moving to an unknown state. Our relationship had become quite fragile, so it seemed an opportune time to perhaps improve our bond.

I'd asked Spirit for guidance as to whether this was a good move. While I was in Sedona with students, I drove into Oak Creek Village to get some gas. A huge banner was strung across the station, *"Austin Cigarettes,"* I'd asked for a sign and Voila! there it was. Later, I was to discover that it was a sign only for me and that Austin Cigarettes, didn't exist. However, the sign served to cement my decision to make the move.

Prior to moving, on impulse, I called the Health Services Institute at Austin Community College to inquire about teaching Reiki and other integrative medicine practices. Right timing, it seems, was at play and my teaching was welcomed! Nursing students could get C.E.U.'s for the classes and the director of the program, Naomi, and her partner also took the classes. I was fortunate with their support, and great enthusiasm on the part of the students, to experience successes.

I was also able to present a talk on Ancient Healing Wisdom for the University of Texas Quest Program. My employment with Williamson County's Health Department gave me a further venue for promoting complimentary health practices. Located in Georgetown, a very conservative area, I was invited to give a lunch time talk in the courthouse on Reiki. Much to almost everyone's surprise, the courtroom presentation was extremely well attended.

This was a nice time of the merger of my avocation and vocation. And, all might have gone on cozily except for September 11, 2001. Our health services program was in large part funded by United Way. The aftermath of which meant our funding was eventually cut. Perhaps sans 9/11 and the dot.com bomb, I may have spent more time in Austin, yet as ever, it was impactful in a compressed timeframe.

Cross Roads Retreat Center and Other Places

As I'd found in other places, I discovered one of my sacred places to go in Texas. I cannot remember who introduced me to this lovely setting and its wondrous labyrinth, I just remember working through the maze and returning many times for solitude and spiritual solace. Surrounded by live oak and an outdoor sanctuary, Cross Roads spoke to my need for a place to go within.

There was also a chapel of some kind near Salado Texas where I enjoyed a wonderful art community thanks to my friend Tricia. I often visited there during my 10 months stay.

Enchanted Rock in Fredericksburg was another spot for meditation and one where I took a visiting student for ceremony. The Texas Hill country has a softness about it that was a comfort among so much machismo energy. Again, I sought a spot in a popular place that as little trafficked to invoke the spirits and learn more about the early immigrants to the lands.

Finally, yet another friend, introduced me to a spot nearer I-10 where a man had reproduced the configurations of Stonehenge England in an open field called Stonehenge II. The sentries guarding Stonehenge II are Easter Island statue replicas. With only us at the time in the vicinity, I could transport myself energetically to the true Stonehenge and a Solstice event out of the time and space continuum.

As an aside, I did get to go bats in Austin; Mexican free-tailed bats that is. One of the major curiosities in March to May, is to stand on the Congress Avenue Bridge at dusk and see nearly a million bats flying to the East replete with the bat scent that can be a bit overwhelming.

Thus, with bats, labyrinths, Stonehenge energy, and a powerful rock, my time in Texas was fruitful and probably lead to one of the last events, a trip to Peru and the re-birth promised by bat energies.

Peru and the Amaru Maru Portal

An opportunity was presented about a possible trip to Peru in conjunction with teaching on the trip. My good friend Richard who I'd ordained in Universal Brotherhood, graciously made it possible for me to make the impactful journey.

If you've never been to Peru and have any way to go, I highly recommend it. The magnificence of the terraced mountains, serene rivers, sacred valleys, colorful native attire, warm gracious people, llamas, and ruins make it a once in a lifetime scenic and spiritually-charged wonder.

14,000 feet can be a challenge for many people, though I navigated that well with my lovely roommate Saundra from Uganda! We drank tons of water while others drank coca tea; we never got sick; many of them did. This trip was free of the famous Amazonian ayahuasca so touted today by many shamanic teachers. The energies were electric enough!

Our excellent host, guide, and shaman, Jorge Delgado, along with the Quechua Shaman, took us to all the usual tourist sites and then, Lake Titicaca and the impactful Amaru Maru Portal. Our group was comprised of some of my students and another couple's students from New York.

Tension developed between the couple and me over promised time for teaching and avoidance of doing specifically that for much of the trip. Jealousy prevailed which later took an ugly turn into what might have been a fatal fall.

Our main base was in Cusco, a lovely city. Food was most agreeable and we experienced a lovely night time ceremony in one of Jorge's friends sacred sites. Vendors followed us everywhere yet goods were most affordable and treasures to remember our time.

All the national monuments or ruins, at that time in Peru, were without facilities. After splendid accommodations in Cusco, a few of our travelers were a bit off put by having an outdoor toilet anywhere that other others could form a blanket of coats to surround one for privacy.

My Spanish held up well and I could follow much of what was said except for Quechua, an unknown language to me. Interpretations were, however, excellent. As we journeyed thorough the state of Cusco and visited all the usual tourist sites, we were also gifted unusual places. Along the Urubamba river in the Sacred Valley, we spent time with a local potter and his family. The warmth of Peru's people was present everywhere we went.

Getting to Ollantaytambo the power of the Apu, Wiracocha, Inti, Pachamama, Chakana etc. began to magnify. If I had not had family to return to, I felt I could live here forever in deep and abiding peace. From here on, and after we'd invoked messages from the gods. in lovely Ollantaytambo, we picked up the train to Machu Picchu.

We stayed in Aguas Caliente, a more tropical locale, below Machu Picchu. It was here that after a day of exploring Machu Picchu and with steady rainy weather, I finally just announced I'd be teaching a class, and did. Despite all the attempts to disrupt opportunities for my teaching by the New York couple, my declaration brought even Jorge to enjoy a class. Jorge very much liked my style and content and promised that if in future I'd bring a select, hand-picked group to Peru, he'd take us to a little known very sacred place that is out of reach for tourists.

The daytime explorations of Machu Picchu were great though it was being in the park at night with just our group that was the most wonderful. Jorge lead us on several other world journeys and trust experiences under a star-light sky that awakened a deep connection with the glory of the Incan Empire and introduced us to supportive guides that were, that night, available to us.

Our other very impactful experience came in Aguas Caliente at his friend Hebert's metaphysical store; again, at night. As we became relaxed and the lights dimmed, Hebert and others played an impressive and evocative concert of musical instruments. Along with chanting and invoking the gods, we journeyed out of the time and space continuum again to places of discovery and personal release from the known. I have a CD of the experience that I've used occasionally with apprentice students. It takes the participant to another realm.

From Machu Picchu, we went to Lake Titicaca and Jorge's very lovely accommodations. The highlight of those days, besides colorful dancers and entertainment, was our journey to the Amaru Maru Portal.

This gateway is off the beaten track and accessible by hiking over some challenging passes and high ridges. As I mentioned earlier, I was experiencing something very untoward from the New York couple, specifically the wife. As we began to navigate what is referred to as the *"Tale of the Puma,"* an extremely narrow high passage, I had a vision of someone falling. It felt like the woman ahead of me. Surprise, I either took her fall or the New Yorker wished one on me. The first 8 feet or so I slide; the next I flew.

As I recall I landed on my hands. Immediately people found a safer passage down to help me. Many started sending energy to me for healing. Because I was not comfortable with all the people's energy, much of my time laying there was spent fending off the sent energy.

Somehow, I got back up, and we continued to the portal. One at a time, we each approached the portal and stood in the gateway, asking for healing, insight, energy or whatever was foremost in our minds. We held our hands on the sides of the portal, closed our eyes and just let the energies carry us.

Back at the Inn, Jorge called on his Curanderos to immediately come and work on me. They plastered a paste called 'chili-chili' all over me and wrapped me in what appeared to be butcher block paper. I was instructed to leave it on until it all fell off.

Amazingly, the next day I could climb the 500 steps on Taquile Island, slowly, and I did reach the top. We also visiting the floating island of Uros. My ankle had appeared to be injured from the fall yet I could enjoy our visitations around Lake Titicaca. Later when I got home and went to my Orthopedic doctors, they were amazed that other than severe bruising all along my spine, no further damage had been experienced.

The last night Jorge took us to a beach somewhere an initiated us into The Brotherhood of the Golden Disc gifting us a necklace to wear that symbolized our initiation. The following day of our departure was a much different experience.

A transportation strike had commenced country wide except for airlines. Though we were right on the border of Bolivia, the decision was made to run the pickets. Our large tourist bus was exchanged for several smaller transport busses. Glass, rocks, and other objects were strewn on much of the road to Juliaca where we'd pickup our plane.

At each juncture, Jorge would get out and negotiate with the strikers. At some point, we arrived at a location with another large tourist bus and re-boarded. Some of the travelers were starting to freak out. I heard the useless, *"We're Americans"* mantra as if that was going to get us out of the situation.

One woman was manifesting so much fear that it was her window that a rock was indeed thrown through. Fortunately, she was not hurt. I calmed down the travelers with some soothing words and we got to Juliaca. Choosing to travel not on main roads, at one point we got stuck in mud and shit.

We gingerly evacuated the bus while the more stalwart were commissioned to push it out of the muck. Standing safely across the street, I burst into laughter at the absurdity of the situation and how poetic justice was being served—being stuck in shit!

We finally reached the airport, traveled to Lima and then on to our respective homes. To this day, I so value the entire Peru adventure and have a sacred altar rug and lovely ancient wall hanging to remind me of its unsurpassed beauty.

When I returned home to the job project whose funds had been suspended, I was laid off. Curiously my boss asked me, *"Are you returning to New Mexico?"* That turned out to be quite prophetic along with enrollment in the Sophia Seminary of the Church of Antioch in Santa Fe.

10 hours of straight driving and I was back to the Land of Entrapment, or so it was called by some people in the know.

CHAPTER IX.
LAND OF ENTRAPMENT

Alaskan Scrimshaw Bear Totem Tusk

Rancho de Los Barrancas

Like the song, Hotel California's lyrics, in New Mexico you can check out but you can never leave. That is still true to this day but more in my heart than physicality. Back to New Mexico I came though, first living outside of Santa Fe in Pojoaque on the res' at Los Barrancas.

On initial impression Los Barrancas was an idyllic spot to land in my revisit to New Mexico. The land was on several acres with about eight houses, a pond with swans, community swimming pool, composting, hen houses, guest house, Yurt, and an active community of people with metaphysical and mystical orientations.

The illusion was short-lived, though the lovely home I rented served me well. It seems there were two warring factions occupying the other homes: the original followers of the founder; and the new people who wanted to change things. Some residents didn't speak to others. So much for joining a community though I'd realized it was the next wave that those of us on a spiritual path needed to embrace.

I ended up working at Los Alamos Laboratory for the security company on a temporary assignment. Not having anything other than a minimal clearance, I had the first time of experiencing no freedom. Once I walked through the heavy metal turnstile and entered the room where I worked, I needed a guard even to go to the bathroom.

Despite the disharmony at Los Barrancas and the restrictions at Los Alamos, my home was just lovely and it was wonderful to walk the pond each day and greet the swans and ducks. The sky was a wonder at night with a canopy of stars and Orion visible most nights. I made one good friend in the complex and we ceremonied together to celebrate the changing sun and moon cycles.

When President Bush declared the preemptive strike on Iraq, the halls were filled with AK7's and tanks with machine gun turrets atop them were parked all along the road, I decided it was time to move on.

The energies of New Mexico also inspired me to move forward with my spiritual work again with the opportunity to become a priest in the Church of Antioch, an independent catholic church.

Sophia Seminary

Admission to the Church of Antioch Sophia Seminary gave me immediate access to a spiritual community even though my dwelling place in Pojoaque had lacked it.

Prior to moving to Santa Fe, I'd had a lengthy conversation with the then Archbishop. Antioch offered what Roman Catholicism lacked for me. It was free of the dogma, progressive, inclusive, and embraced women as ordained priests. As I wanted to expand my ministry, it seemed a wonderful option.

I enjoyed my early studies and connected with a wonderful group of people at my first annual convention for the school. In addition to the school, I trained to serve on the altar using traditional smudging, holy water, and communion. We also had a discussion and healing night that I could participate in as an active member and healer. For a time, Antioch and the community served me very well and gave me instant access to a community of like-minded people. I made many great friends.

The rub? The leader of the church, the archbishop, was a lecher and everyone knew it even the rest of the bishops. His behavior was so inappropriate with women and so base in nature that I came to a point there I could no longer be affiliated with him and have my reputation tied to such disgusting behavior.

When I shared the whys of my leaving with one of the women bishops that I greatly admired, she pleaded with me to stay as she felt the organization needed more strong women like me. I was flattered a bit yet knew that if people of influence in Santa Fe knew of the main bishop's lechery, that impression would taint me.

It was a gut-wrenching decision to leave as I felt such camaraderie in the organization; something I'd been missing in most of my life. Some friendships withered because of my decision and my reluctance to reveal the real reason for my departure.

In the end, I only stayed in touch with a select few among them a dear, dear friend who had Stage IV Ovarian Cancer, Francesca. One of my gifts of my Santa Fe time was being available to her for healings before and after chemotherapy. With the work, we did together, and the congregation's prayers, she lived four years after the diagnosis which MD Anderson Doctors told her was a miracle.

Apprentices and Teaching

As I disengaged myself from the Sophia Divinity School, it freed me up to resume shamanic teaching and apprenticeships.

I was back in the groove of shamanic work and it felt right and energetically a good choice. Many people were still attracted to the work and classes began. As with other experiences of teaching, the larger classes eventually boiled down to smaller groups that were committed to going the distance with the Masters of Shamanic Arts.

It was my privilege to even work with some students who'd already worked with 'big name' teachers yet found my work to be of great benefit with bonuses of acquired skills and knowledge.

While the energies of Santa Fe had slightly diminished from the early days of commutes to work with don Miguel, there was still an electric charge there and the magnificent light that is purported to be only one of two places in the world with this light-conducive to creativity and spiritual awakening.

My small duplex held many teachings and ceremonies during my six years there (split with one year in Albuquerque). I had a large group that developed mostly of Curanderismo students from Albuquerque that I also taught. Students who were most dedicated commuted to Santa Fe when I returned and we culminated their Masters of Shamanic Arts Program in picturesque Dixon. What a magical place that was for the culminating ceremony.

The setting included a stone pool in which I performed the beautiful Water Ritual of Birth for each apprentice. We had magical walking paths to explore and connect with the elements. Our three days culminated with the ritual Fire Ceremony for graduation which was phenomenal.

As it happened that the weekend was also Samhain, we did a ceremony to connect with a deceased member of each apprentice's family and everyone had a most significant contact.

With all our power tools from our other intensive workshops, the magnificent high desert setting, the thinning veils of Samhain, the mystical appearance of significant animals, the pool and the fire, this last Albuquerque apprenticeship group experienced stepping into their own power.

I also had individual apprentices in Santa Fe during this corridor. One comes to mind who shall remain unnamed for privacy. That said, here was a woman who came to me with no confidence and direction in her life and has gone on to start her own successful businesses, introduce products and move gracefully and powerfully into the practice of ceremony and shamanic celebration.

CHAPTER X:
HIGH AND LOW DESERTS

Peruvian Rattle, Owl Rattle, Scorpio, Water Serpent

Prescott

The siren's call had sounded again after six year's return to New Mexico, a short-term failed marriage, and an inner knowing that my energies were needed elsewhere. The decision to move dependent on getting into an art show whose deadline had passed. Always, I was looking for signs to support my inklings.

I got into the show and decided that Prescott would be my next adventure. I'd visited it many times when I lived in Sedona and always found it quite comfortable. This small city reminded me of the many mid-western towns that my family had lived in during our vagabond childhood.

Connections were made magically the very first time I visited the Unity congregation. The woman sitting next to me commented, *"you are a healer; a shaman."* I wondered how on earth she knew that. Then, perhaps I might not have wondered as there is some energy exchange that takes place between sensitive people that seems to announce one another.

She invited me to a weekly women's sacred group that became a mainstay of connection and spiritual sustenance during the two years that I stayed in Prescott.

My years there were occupied by running a front office for a network chiropractor, conducting the moon ceremonies, teaching classes, being a very active part of the arts community, and enjoying a menagerie of animals.

Animal medicine seemed a huge part of the Prescott

experience. I lived at the top of a hill with a large vacant lot next to me; perhaps that is what made the animals free to roam. Javelina were frequent visitors even during ceremony on my patio. I distinctly remember one participant being concerned about safety as their crowd cruised by and I assured her that their limited sight would not be an issue.

For one Summer Solstice, a large unidentified, snake crawled up on my patio as my brother and I sat watching it. It didn't have a rattle on the tail so we decided it was harmless and just enjoyed our special visitor who coiled around the legs of the chairs entertaining us.

One night I returned from a dress up event and a little skunk greeted me as I approached the door. Not knowing whether the young ones sprayed or not, and it was so adorable, I told the little one that it was fun seeing him or her and scurried into the house.

Another afternoon as I approached my home late in the day, a small doe was languishing on the gravel in front. She was a bit shy and cautious as I approached the door. I assured her that it was OK if she stayed a while.

My most impactful visitor was probably the mountain lion that I approached one day as I was walking around the complex. He had his back to me as I realized who he was across the field. Very carefully, I stepped back between the cars and quietly walked backwards to my home.

So, with all this medicine I was gifted magic, adaptability, strong connections, loyalty, a bit of trickery, transmutation, reputation, gentleness, and leadership; powerful symbols. Apparently celestial influences drew these animals to me and we all lived in harmony with one another.

As with other places I'd lived after New Mexico, I found the magical places in Prescott to perform ceremony which had by then become the hallmark of my work. Thumb Butte was within my view daily from my patio and the magnificent sunsets added to creating an aura of mysticism around my immediate neighborhood.

My friend, Denise, introduced me to Chapel Rock, a retreat center with a lovely outdoor altar and palpable feeling of sacredness. Granite Dells was another sacred place to commune with the wonder of tall rocks as their own brand of standing people and wisdom keepers.

Community became a major gift of the time spent in Northern Arizona. Teaching was somewhat limited by the highly conservative nature of the old guard in the city. Although Prescott College students were very progressive and embracing latter day hippie ways, the greater community was not as open to what I might have offered.

It was a pleasant respite until the after effects of the crash of 2008 caught up to the town and it was time to come down from the mountain and get among the greater people again.

Not receiving a clear message about my next step, I decided to return to Tucson. I knew whatever it would offer me, it was a doable place and one that I was very familiar with.

Back to Tucson

I chose the fall to return thinking it best to ease back into the fire that is the hallmark of Sonoran summers. I'd missed the smell of sage and the awesome and stark beauty of the desert, it seemed. Ever since the first tumbleweed blew across the highway on my first trip west and the first butte rose before me, I've loved the desert. It is not an easy love affair.

Fire is the element most prevalent in the Sonoran Desert with a heat buildup in the summer time that forces one's transformation. Though the spikes and thorns of multitude of cactus keep admirers at a distance, the blooms unfolding quench the thirst of parched occupants.

And, so it was that I returned to the staggeringly tall sentinels, Saguaro, in Old Pueblo to await a clearer instruction as to my next relocation. It was a long wait as it turned out; five years.

Electro-magnetic energy prevails in our deserts along with Fuji color skies. It seems my energies are always more easily aroused when I among the cactus. The balanced yin and yang of Tucson's mountains compliment that certain charge that I feel when I returned.

It was an easy transition being back as I still had connections there; starting a moon group was one of my first ventures. The crazy population burst that Raytheon had caused when I first left, had leveled out. There was, however, a significant difference in the spiritual community.

While somewhat of an anomaly being a shamanic practitioner when I lived here in the late 90's, the market was a bit glutted now. Advertisements abounded for this and that shaman and practice. I had to carve out my niche.

This gave me time to think and that lead to my more active writing phase and the publication of my first book. Early on I didn't have the space to resume the intensives I'd fostered previously, so teaching venues became of some import.

As my Moon Meetup developed, a group of women began to coalesce around ceremony, art, and community. We were still able to experience a little magic with Solstice and Equinox ceremonies at Agua Caliente and Sanctuary Cove. A labyrinth was now built at the cove and I proved one could walk on hot rocks to experience it. A clear demonstration of mind over matter!

Somewhere in this period, I connected with Oasis Lifelong Learning and began teaching a series of classes for them along with fostering meditation at my apartment complex.

2012 and the Birth of the New Earth

Through my previous involvement with the 11:11 Gateway, I'd known about the Mayan Calendar shift due in December 2012. I'd never seen it as an end of all things and that proved a good take as we are now clearly past that end date!

I connected with The Shift Network and Barbara Marx Hubbard's New Birth of Earth focus and Agents of Conscious Evolution in early 2012. The on-line training at it's very best connected us in small triads with people around the world who were wanting to be part of a mammoth evolutionary shift in human consciousness.

Early on, I organized the Southern Arizona participants into a group to explore ways that we might contribute to the efforts and culminating celebration on December 22, 2012. One of the self-professed board members deigned to join our first meeting although she stood the whole time and left early on. We were not enthralled with her posturing. She also failed to share that she already had a plan of action. We did not find out about the latter until some months into the nine-month's preparation.

As most of us, over time, came to conclude that we enjoyed Barbara and her vision, we struggled with The Shift Movement. It seemed to be espousing 21st century concepts using 20th century outmoded methods. Incongruity came to my mind and I chose to go no further than the first training and a few free offerings, which in general were just adverts for the new age famous to rake in more bucks.

I realize this sounds a little harsh. Given that our very first call had 800 amazing people from around the world with a collective talent pool available to support the mission, it just seemed so old school to recycle all the new age gurus who made big money in the hay day of the new age.

We met regularly to develop a plan for how we might impact the Southern Arizona community. It was finally decided that we would offer ceremonies at the Solstice and

Equinox times to educate people on the concept, mission, and share the power of circle.

As the in-house ceremonialist, I developed the actual ceremonies for our celebrations. We staged these at venues around Tucson and enjoyed somewhat limited, yet enthusiastic, attendees. We also took this work to another group in town that was looking for ways to build community. The latter group, male-dominated, expressed distaste for ceremony and that was the end of that.

For the culmination on the evening of December 21st overnight into the morning of the 22nd, I sponsored an all-women's incredible ceremony, sharing, and awakening at my new property near the Tucson Mountains.

Magdala Sanctuary

That brings me to the inaugural phase of Magdala Sanctuary! It had always been my dream to have a place that was named Magdala Sanctuary in memory of Mary of Magdala. I'd imagined it in the country somewhere near water with a chapel and shared land. Though that dream was not realized, another emerged unexpectedly in 2012 when my youngest son and I decided to jointly own a home in Tucson.

As Spirit sometimes delivers something even better, so it was that one of the last properties I viewed in a long search was the one. The house was unspectacular though pleasant with a few good cosmetic improvements. Old growth Palo Verde and Mesquite added a lot to the first take. It was the large back yard that sealed the deal.

As I stepped through the screen door off the patio, there was a large stone raised platform to my right. It had a dilapidated spa on it. I climbed the steps and there in full splendor, short doors away from mine, was a large expanse of the Tucson Mountains gleaming in the sunlight to the West. Turning around at the top of the platform, I could see the Rincon's, Santa Rita's, and the Santa Catalina mountain ranges. The possibilities seemed open. This would be the altar and stage for many, many ceremonies.

During my two years hosting Magdala Sanctuary, I was privileged to share the space with regular new and full moon ceremonies, a large African/Hindu/Celtic wedding, guests at the Airbnb, apprentice students and students from out of town seeking a more intense experience of some aspect of shamanism.

Being in a primarily Latino neighborhood, I never felt any untoward reactions from my shamanistic practices that were evident in the back yard. In fact, for the wedding, I took time to visit the neighbors on either side of me, across the street and behind me. There only comment was *"Will we be able to hear the music?"* That was meant as a good thing, something they were looking forward to and they expressed no issues with however long it lasted. The next day they voiced approval of the whole event especially the music!

The yard was strung with lights from the house to the trees. The musicians played African drums, a digeridoo, and we even had a Native American flutist. The ceremony included a traditional Hindu Fire Ceremony at the fire pit and the fountain sang in the background. It was the largest event I would host there and fulfilled my dream of offering a sanctuary for life events.

Twice monthly people from all over Tucson and as far south as Tubac, came to Magdala Sanctuary for the moon ceremonies and meditations. House guests also joined us from time to time. The energies were always flowing easily for me as they tend to do in the electric energies of the Southwest and mountains.

For Mary Magdalene's feast day on July 22nd, we had a very special ceremony for women moon celebrators and former students. Crystal bowls were brought to magnify the sound and penetration of the drums, rattles, etc. The bowls along with high quality tuning forks went right into the core of each attendant. I'd divined a special Goddess for each woman and it seemed I was right on target for all.

The only down side of my location had nothing to do with the property or home, it was a deep prejudice against the southwest and south side of Tucson. That prejudgment began to show up on both sides of the equation. When I moved there, it was still predominantly Latino. The housing crash, and foreclosed properties, began to draw non-Hispanics to the area.

As the neighborhoods were becoming more gentrified, I watched particularly young Latinos begin to express dislike and distain towards whites as employed clerks in stores and restaurants. What a shame it seemed to me. Yet I could see where they felt the encroachment was monetarily motivated and changing the tenor or tempo of an area they'd long called home.

Because of the reputation of the area and distance from the Catalina foothills where I'd formerly lived, I just never seemed as successful as I'd imagined in drawing more people to Magdala Sanctuary. Daunting as that was, at times, there was a redeeming quality that kept my spirits up and introduced me to a community that I felt at home with.

Tubac Consciousness Group

On a whim, I'd ventured down to Amado, near Tubac, to attend a Center for Spiritual Living one day. I'd explored several of the similar communities in Tucson and yet didn't feel a connection there. The welcoming of this community was phenomenal and I enjoyed the wit and intelligence of the minister.

Initially, I'd visit on occasion with weeks in between. What thrilled me is that people there remembered me each time I attended. It was through folks that I met at the center, that I connected with the consciousness group in Tubac.

For many months and many miles, I drove 45 minutes each way to participate in the group. What an amazing group of spiritual people! There were so very many gifted, grounded, spiritual, and talented men and women that it was a joy to do the long commute.

Through that involvement, I would teach a basic shamanism course; present a talk from one of my books; do a poetry reading at a book store; had my jewelry in an art shop and performed a well-attended Equinox ceremony. It seemed that what I'd perceived as lessor involvement in Tucson was well made up for in Tubac.

And, then as groups sometime evolve, ours did. There was a divide between two leaders-one former, one current. It seemed people felt a need to choose sides—always a divisive posture and a most unfortunate one in a group exploring consciousness. Perhaps this is inevitable until we all finally retire our egos and find our way to true heart-centered living.

For a time, I'd considered relocating to Tubac. The groups demise and split moved me away from that decision. As the costs of maintaining a 40-year-old house on limited income began to manifest the ugly reality, I felt it was time to move on. The old restlessness that had often preceded my moves was with me and resource seemed to be withering.

Yet, I'd still not received a clear message as to where I was to go. When an offer came in on the house one day after listing, I was torn. It was a contingency offer with a rent back. Ultimately, I felt the energies I'd created and all the improvements would be at risk. The decision to decline, however, came in the most unlikely way.

I decided to Google the couple. To my amazement there was not one shred of presence in any of the social media and the only thing I could conform, was that they were married. That decision kept me in Tucson another few months yet provided at least some impetus to make a move in the direction of the Pacific Northwest.

CHAPTER XI.
FULL CIRCLE

Cross Woman by my late friend, Francesca

Winds

From Santa Ana's, to Chinook, to Haboob, to Derecho's and more, winds have blown into and out of my life. As the clever North Wind that blew in the movie *Chocolat* and carried Vianne and her daughter Anouk to their next port of call, it seems it was not satisfied in my life either. Trees began to fall on my land and, for me, they were clear messages, leave, sooner than later.

Ashland

As before, I was looking for signs as to where this wind was taking me. My computer guru had moved to Ashland and loved it. Then I met a metaphysical man who surprisingly, or not, was determined to move to Ashland as he'd heard great things about it. He was weeks away from leaving when we visited Kartchner Caverns. Caves have always held a fascination for me. I feel they can provide deep answers to things that appear to be more subconscious than conscious.

I began to explore it [sic: Ashland] as a possible new venue. Part of that discovery process was to connect with the metaphysical community. I read about the minister at Unity in Ashland who was also a shamanic practitioner and teacher and contacted her.

We had an amazing conversation and she shared with me her intention to build an earth temple there. The project appealed to me. I felt it would be a great connection place and provide an opportunity to make immediate connections and contribute.

I might have visited the area before making a final decision but my neck went into distress and I was forced to spend considerable time getting treatment and therapy for it. My friend had made the move and was touting how great he was finding the community. The other friend also sang its praises. With the house sale and closings, along with the healing, there just was no time to do anything except move on.

I'd thought for some time that the Pacific Northwest was calling me back and knew that I'd exceeded my 40 days and nights in the desert; water was calling. At the same, time things in Tucson seemed to be shutting down and it felt right, though I was time pressed, to move on up the road.

Additionally, I'd located a doctor in Bend, Oregon who was doing stem cell therapy and hoped that I might take advantage of that as I had a few shekels from the home sale.

Trusting that I was making the right decision, I chose Ashland, I believe some part of me had an inner hesitancy that I just opted to override. Truth be told, I know better than to override intuition, yet indeed it appeared when all was said and done, that is what I did.

It was smooth driving all the way which was encouraging. I arrived late at night and was so thankful to have a place to stay with my computer guru friend, Lisa. Her roommate was out of town so it allowed space for me to rest and find housing.

The first day we sat down by the creek in a slight wind taking in all the beautiful blossoms, eating at a lovely restaurant, and visiting the Sunday fair along the creek.

By the next morning, I was sicker than a dog from the beautiful blossoms. Seems I was having a major allergy attack which quickly moved into bronchitis and asthma. This did not portend well for my initial exposure to Ashland. I had to go to emergency care immediately and my host ended up taking care of me for several days until I could even get out of bed.

When I could be up and about again, I began the search for housing. The second doubt set in as I discovered that there was only 1% of housing available and an aggressive market in which one had to be the very first person at a place to secure it.

For almost three weeks, I staggered out each day after religiously hunting Craigslist to find a new home. In the meantime, I visited the Unity. To my surprise the minister hardly remembered our conversation or the book I'd sent her. She promised to be in touch about the earth project and yet in the 8 months I lived there never followed up with me. The general community, at that center, was a bit too far out for me too. I just didn't feel a connection.

This became a pattern in Ashland, initial welcoming and then doors closing. I started a Moon Group Meetup with marginal success. Joined a drumming group. Became a member of two art society's neither of which were welcoming. I felt that whatever Ashland had once been in terms of special energy, it had changed. It felt exclusive not inclusive. Moreover, whatever initial energies had been present, they were now most definitely skewed.

If I hadn't had the friendships I'd had before I came, it might have been incredibly lonely. Every other friendship or group that I tried to either join or start, just didn't come together. Always there was the promise of what might be just beyond the reach of fruition.

I'd finally secured housing in Talent, between Ashland and Medford. Despite all the Ashland folk looking down on Medford, I spent much more time there ultimately than I did in Ashland.

There were ceremonies I facilitated and I did perform two weddings in Spanish during my short stay. My energies came alive doing the ceremonies and a following developed until I decided to charge a stipend. That was the proverbial kiss of death except for a stalwart few. What a concept, ask for a bit of compensation for a wonderful teaching and ceremony. What was I thinking?

It was the fires and smoke that finally drove me out at my doctor's orders. My C.O.P.D. returned and I was constantly having to be on steroids. The diagnosis also allowed me to get out of my one-year lease. Friends of mine so loved my apartment that they rented it the day I moved out.

Ashland became the same money pit that had been Sedona and for about the same length of time. Not that it was all bad, it is lovely, lovely country in terms of just the visual agreeableness. I enjoyed spending time with Lisa and Darrell. The vineyards were wonderful and in bucolic settings. I spent time with one of my first cousins in Medford which was, I believe, a good connection and contact point for him.

Yet, my lungs and pocketbook said enough! I began to explore where else I might choose. Bellingham began to send out an energetic beacon and being one hour from my youngest son and grandson in Vancouver, I began to explore it.

This time, I visited twice before making the choice to move yet again; two times in one year. Spirit was supporting this move however. Each time I was in a doubting mood about the choice, a beautiful rainbow broke out across the sky. Rainbows have always held a specialness for me both as a child and later as a Rainbow Girl in my teens.

Bellingham

I found in Bellingham all the connections that had just eluded me in Ashland. Within my second visit, I was in an art show. I connected with three different metaphysical centers. Found a new friend somehow through Facebook and everyone was welcoming and helpful. In this regard, it reminded me a bit of Prescott yet much more liberal and set against a beautiful bay.

Housing came quickly and easily. I found an apartment for seniors, my first experience, with a corner unit on the top floor. It could not have been a better choice for me. Again, I felt welcome and almost instantly knew three or four people in the first week including my neighbor Susan across the hall.

In the Center for Spiritual Living, I found a kindred soul in the minister. I enjoyed her talks and perspectives. For a time, I tried to promote a class and book sales but I was apparently too new for an established congregation to embrace me and the class did not happen there. However, the introductory offerings generated interest that later turned into a year-long class that I held.

I love the water and being so close to the bay. The vastness and movement were much missed in my life after many years in desert climes. Even the wild winter storms have an appeal. The rain does not phase me as even on the rainiest day the sun will break through for a time.

Another class developed teaching meditation for residents of my complex. I've now expanded that to teaching the same class for another senior complex. A program at WWU's Academy for Lifelong Learning embraced my teaching and I am offering a class for them.

I have weddings lined up for next year and continue exploring the area and finding the sacred places to energize and be at peace enfolded in the emerald green. I'm expanding my photography repertoire to take in this beauty.

Art sales have been successful thus far in different venues here and I'm connecting increasingly with women in the community and with a wonderful group of metaphysicians. I feel good here! The proximity to my son and grandson are the icing on the cake and I feel that here, in Bellingham, I can land for a while.

My first year closed with co-facilitating a meditation, ceremony, and community social event entitled Solstice Shower of Light! My friends, Lisa, Jim, Sara and I made it a memorable evening of embodying the light within and without.

I've come full circle being back in the Pacific Northwest after 25 years. The beauty of the indigenous art called me long, long ago over a Kwakiutl Mask at the Denver Art Museum. It touched something deep in me that spoke of home. I shared that moment with a man who was the great love of my life. We moved from Denver to Portland Oregon and began our dance. That relationship changed my life in many ways. Perhaps it was the first part of a movement that pointed me in a different direction. The ten-year relationship produced a beautiful child and a major alteration of mindset. Our paths converged and then directed us apart; both of us modified along with our histories.

Many years in between, with two oceans and many deserts, have called me back to the art and rhythm of these coastal tribes. Their drum beat, carvings, teal, and salmon colors has lured me back to my destiny.

The hidden whys of my journey will be revealed to me in good time. Of that I am very sure as I've learned to trust Divine plan. There is no doubt that I will be able to add value, nurture and be nurtured. I am grateful to be here.

We all ultimately do dance to a whispered voice. The challenge is to open our inner hearing and follow the call. It may be soft or incredibly loud. We've just to listen and know when and where we are destined to step onto the dance floor of our life purpose and trust the movement. When we do, our life becomes dynamic and filled with wonder and discovery.

Passion

Passion has broad hips and deep absorbing eyes. She is an artful dancer whose moves undulate like the sea. When she lifts her veils, and twirls you can feel the vibration of life's rhythms in every fiber of your being.

Passion and her cousin Sensuality host a celebratory ritual each Spring Equinox to awaken dormant dreamers and re-calibrate earth's resonance. All the Qualities are invited--it is, after all, a passion play.

The Gossips say that Passion is pansexual. Her sensuous mouth coos love and promise to all who dare skirt her fires. In her kaleidoscope eyes unfold new worlds. Consummation is her specialty.

Asked once if she is fickle she replied, *"I cannot be contained."* The music of Passion's voice has engulfed more than a few faithless lovers. Her cantata "Communion" sounds a purifying release for believers in her transformative powers.

Passion is a frequent visitor at Ecstasy's Mountain Inn where she and The Wind restore his soul.

[Written by me many years ago, as an addition to Ruth Gendler's book, The Qualities.]

ABOUT THE AUTHOR

Amari Magdalena is an elder wisdom keeper, master healer, artist, and author of several books on aspects of shamanism. She founded The Institute for Shamanic Synthesis in 1995 to foster sharing ancient wisdom tools for modern high stress living. She began her sojourn into shamanism in 1990 and has been teaching, writing, lecturing and practicing shamanism for 25 years. Magdalena has been privileged to know and work with the late Elena Avila, Woman Who Glows in the Dark; Don Miguel Ruiz, The Four Agreements; Mother Sarita Vasquez; Jorge Luis Delgado; Barbara Marx-Hubbard, Birth 2012 and Beyond; and multiple practitioners of cross-cultural shamanism here and abroad.

Coming full-circle in 2015 by moving back to the Pacific Northwest, Amari feels complete with her long vision quest in desert landscapes. She continues to provide spiritual succor through the concept of Magdala Sanctuary, providing space for individual and group studies and ceremonies.

Magdalena loves to express her passion for art in photography and jewelry design.

She performs weddings and life ceremonies (http://www.soulmateceremonies).

Amari offers individual and group teaching and workshops at various venues in Washington State and is available for programs throughout the U.S. and abroad. Over her 26 years of teaching, she has been honored to apprentice 22 people and teach hundreds of other students seeking inspiration through Earth-based traditions. Amari also facilitates private healing sessions, consultations, and readings in person, on Skype, Facetime or on Google +.

Magdalena is mother of four children and grandmother to their nine offspring. She is currently working on two other books: an autobiography and a book on meditation using shamanic tools.

If you would like to contact her, please write to:

shamanicsynthesis@yahoo.com

Calls are welcomed from 9 am to 6 pm Monday through Friday Pacific Time. 541-591-6503.

Please visit her websites:

http://www.instituteforshamanicsynthesis.com

http://amarimagdalena.blogspot.com/

http://www.facebook.com/magdalasanctuary

http://www.facebook.com/instituteforshamanicsynthesis

https://www.facebook.com/Medicineware-Artistry-by-Amari-103708339706656/

https://www.etsy.com/il-en/shop/Medicineware

http://www.soulmateceremonies.com

http://www.pinterest.com/amarimagdalena/

https://www.linkedin.com/pub/amari-magdalena/11/58/a0a

GLOSSARY OF TERMS

Curanderismo-Healing practices of Mesoamericans.

Dance-The movement of our lives: sometimes conscious; at other times, not.

Journeying-Shamanic technique for traveling to three worlds, upper-middle-lower, for information and healing.

Kiva-A Ceremonial Chamber.

Limpia-Ritual cleansing with an egg, smudging and agua bendita.

Nagual-Magical or non-ordinary reality; shapeshifter.

Recapitulation-Method for retrieving lost pieces of energy over a lifetime.

Shamanism-Ancient practices that believe that all things in the manifest world are sacred.

Sipapu-Center of the Kiva where Spirits enter and leave.

Tonal-Ordinary reality; time/space continuum.

Vision Quest-Time out, especially in nature, for one to access inner wisdom and gain power.

Walk-In-A Soul that is assuming the body of another soul who is choosing to leave this incarnation.

RECOMMENDATIONS

Here are some websites that I feel you will find valuable on several levels:

http://secretsofafairygodmother.com/

http://inquirewithin.com/

http://www.mastersofthejourney.com/

http://harmonyrosewellness.com/mycomama-medicinals/

http://www.shamanichypnosis.com

http://www.thespiritedwoman.com

https://www.facebook.com/Tom-Blue-wolf-132164856819715/

http://onetribetrading.com/

http://www.thrivemovement.com/

http://riseupthemovie.com/

https://www.joycefglick.com

Ceremony in Sedona

BE STILL, BE SILENT

AMARI MAGDALENA

Made in the USA
Lexington, KY
15 July 2017